THE USER'S GUIDE
TO THE
ENVIRONMENT

THE
USER'S GUIDE
TO THE
ENVIRONMENT

JOHN McCORMICK

**KOGAN
PAGE**

For Lesley

First published in Great Britain in 1985 by
Kogan Page Limited
120 Pentonville Road, London N1 9JN

Copyright © John McCormick 1985

British Library Cataloguing in Publication Data

McCormick, John, *1954* –
   The user's guide to the environment.
   1. Conservation of natural resources – Amateurs
   manuals
   I. Title
   333.7′ 2   S938

   ISBN 0-85038-950-X

Printed and bound in Great Britain by
Billing & Sons Ltd, Worcester

CONTENTS

ACKNOWLEDGEMENTS

Volumes have been written and said about what is happening to the environment: about the over-consumption and waste of natural resources, the lack of concern for the costs of the consumer way of life, and about the effects of badly planned development.

The solutions to many of the problems are now well known, and have been widely discussed, but there is a difference between word and deed. Much has been said about what governments could and should be doing to tackle the problems at source, but the role of the individual has too often been overlooked.

The User's Guide to the Environment is an attempt to begin putting the record straight. The idea for the book was influenced by my own experience in the environmental movement, by the reading I have done and the people I have met. The information upon which it is based is, by necessity, a synthesis of the research of organizations and individuals over several decades. I hope their role is adequately reflected in the text.

More immediately, I am indebted to several people who gave up valuable time to read and comment on sections of the book. Bill Adams (Downing College, Cambridge), David Baldock (Earth Resources Research and IIED), James Deane (Earthscan), Philip Lowe (University College London), Chris Rose (Friends of the Earth) and Lloyd Timberlake (Earthscan) all made many useful suggestions on chapters within their areas of expertise or interest. Gerald Foley and Robbie Robertson read through the entire manuscript, and took time to discuss many of the ideas with me. Loulou Brown edited the book with commitment, working to a very tight schedule. Any errors or omissions should not, however, reflect on anyone but myself.

John McCormick
London, January 1985

INTRODUCTION

'Every morning, most of Britain's 37 million urban dwellers wake to an alarm clock which has been assembled half the world away with components from around the globe. Many of the clothes they wear and much of the breakfast they consume will come from cash crops grown in Third World countries, perhaps in competition with local food production. They ride to factories, shops and offices on fuel from the North Sea, use paper from the trees of Northern Europe and work at benches and desks made from the wood of tropical forests where one species is extinguished every 24 hours. During one day, each individual will use 120 litres of water and together they will produce, from their homes alone, 50,000 tonnes of solid waste, most of which will be thrown onto the land around the cities where they live. Yet urban society remains largely ignorant of the scale, diversity and consequences of this resource consumption'

From 'The Livable City', Part 2 of *The Conservation and Development Programme for the UK: A Response to the World Conservation Strategy* (1983)

The environmental crisis is all around us. It is in the air we breathe, in the food we eat and in the water we drink. It is in deforestation, in too much traffic on roads, in eroded soils, in Third World food shortages, in derelict land, and in wasted natural resources. It affects everyone.

Yet for most people the environmental crisis remains a distant, almost intangible, problem. Many remain oblivious to its implications, and others may feel powerless to act. The causes and the solutions are too often portrayed as being beyond the sphere of the individual. Multinationals are blamed for exploiting Third World resources. Industry carries the can for pollution. Farmers are blamed for the deterioration of the British countryside. Oil companies are held responsible for oil spills.

The effect of all this has been to make people feel like bystanders at disasters not of their making. Yet while governments and industry are not blameless, neither are they entirely to blame. They represent the free market society, whose basic unit is the individual consumer. The consumer is at the peak of a pyramid of demand which is the key to present industrial and agricultural policy. Consumer demand helps decide how much food is grown and how it is processed, how many cars are built and how many scrapped, how much energy is generated (and by what means), how much forest is logged, and more.

Consumers are users, the opposite of producers. The consumer society was born in the affluence of the 1950s and 1960s, when Europe and North America enjoyed economic growth, and people had jobs, expanding leisure time and disposable income. For many people, luxury joined – and often replaced – necessity as a motive for ownership. Consumption grew as it had never grown before.

The environmental consequences have been three-fold. Firstly, the concentration of wealth and consumption in the North has put considerable stress on the environment of those African, Asian and Latin American countries which are the source of many of the world's natural resources. Europeans and Americans now consume most of the world's food, energy, wood, minerals and other resources. The 1980 *World Conservation Strategy* warns that 'it is essential that the affluent constrain their demands on resources, and preferably reduce them, shifting some of their wealth to assisting the deprived'.[1]

Secondly, many of the methods used to exploit, process and consume resources have negative side-effects. Road traffic pollutes the atmosphere because there are insufficient exhaust emission controls. When forests are cleared for agriculture or logging, natural habitat and wildlife is destroyed. Poorly planned irrigation can destroy good farmland by saturating or salinizing soil.

Thirdly, many natural resources are wasted and used inefficiently. Only 12 per cent of the petrol put into cars is converted into useful motive power. Most of the energy used to heat British homes seeps through uninsulated walls, windows and roofs. Every year British households throw away 43 million tonnes of food, paper, glass, metal and textiles. In *The Energy Question*, Gerald Foley rightly argues that 'eliminating waste should be the first priority in any society. It should not require an atmosphere of crisis to justify it. But prosperity has conditioned people into believing that avoiding wastefulness is something to be done only in times of emergency'.[2]

One of the fundamental causes of the environmental crisis is that we know too little about the effects of our actions and demands on the environment. The *World Conservation Strategy* notes the prevailing 'lack of awareness of the benefits of conservation and of its relevance to everyday concerns'.[3] Robert Allen, compiler of the Strategy, points out that 'living resources are being destroyed because people do not see that it is in their interests not to destroy them'.[4]

For example, few people would disagree that wildlife faces serious threats all over the world, but equally few would accept – or perhaps realize – their direct responsibility. It is usual to accuse government, industrialists, or unscrupulous hunters and traders, of destroying wildlife habitat by clearing forests, over-fishing oceans, damming rivers, polluting lakes and the air. Yet much of this is done in the name of consumer demand. Norman Myers suggests in *The Sinking Ark* that 'if [affluent-world citizens] truly wish to allow living space for millions of species that existed on the planet before man got on to his hind legs, they will find that entails not only a soft-hearted feeling in support of wildlife, but a hard-nosed commitment to attempt new lifestyles. While they shed a tear over the demise of tropical moist forests with their array of species, they might go easy on the Kleenex'.[5]

Many peoples' demands are dictated by their existing standard of living and by what they regard as their immediate needs. The more the demands of the affluent society are satisfied, the more new ones are created. The free-enterprise system encourages this by convincing people that they have greater needs than they really have, and that they need products and services they could in fact do without. Credit encourages people to live beyond their means. The market exploits the short-term needs of consumers and anticipates their long-term future 'needs', many of which are artificial.

In *The Affluent Society*, J K Galbraith observes that 'consumer wants can have bizarre, frivolous, or even immoral origins, and an admirable case can still be made for a society that seeks to satisfy them. But the case cannot stand if it is the process of satisfying wants that creates the wants'.[6] As long as demands are created, governments will argue that resource exploitation must continue, and sometimes even be stepped up. If, on the other hand, demand falls (as it has in Britain for food and energy), then unchanging government policy becomes increasingly indefensible.

There is still a deeply held belief that conservation blocks progress. Governments, industry and agriculture often take this view. Perhaps it is a legacy from the pre-conservation era when preservation was the ruling philosophy, dictating that nature had to be preserved at all costs, whatever the economic argument for its exploitation. Preservationists came to be seen by developers as Mother Grundies who were anti-progress. There will always be a moral argument for the protection of nature but, in a hard-nosed society where progress is measured in economic development, very few governments or planners are going to accept the moral arguments. When natural resources are at stake, it has always been the hard economic arguments that have won the day. The environmental movement recognized this in the 1960s, and conservation replaced preservation as the favoured solution.

Conservation does *not* mean going without, rationing communities, making major sacrifices or imposing universal asceticism. It does not mean using resources frugally or not at all. It *does* mean using resources rationally and economically. It means making adjustments rather than sacrifices. The lifestyle of the affluent makes unreasonable and often unnecessary demands on natural resources and the environment, mainly because unlimited exploitation is seen as the basis of a good standard of living. But such an argument is both irrational and unsustainable. Unlimited consumption cannot last, because the earth cannot cope. Conservation means maintaining present lifestyles while using resources more efficiently, thereby reducing the cost to the environment. It means living off the interest (the produce of natural systems) rather than the capital (the systems themselves). If consumerism is demanding the impossible of resources and the environment, then conservation is demanding the possible.

We have made adjustments already, for instance in the way we use oil. In 1973, oil consumption was growing steadily. In Britain it had grown by 140 per cent in 12 years, in France by 330 per cent and in Japan by 670 per cent. Then came the oil price rises of the 1970s, and the world was obliged to curb its consumption. So instead of continuing to rise, consumption has fallen by 28 per cent in Britain, by 19 per cent in France and by 22 per cent in Japan. And this has been achieved without any major effect on our way of life. Twenty years ago in the United States, vast gas-guzzling cars were the norm. Today, small and fuel-efficient cars have become both fashionable and practical.

Food provides another example. The mounting evidence of the past decade that much of our diet is unhealthy and linked to the higher than average incidence of particular diseases has encouraged many people to rethink their diets and to eat healthier food. The health risks associated with smoking have meant that the habit, previously thought to be socially acceptable, is now regarded as unsociable and unacceptable. The American environmentalist Lester Brown writes of the irony in the fact that 'declines in consumption of some items among the affluent often correlate with improvements in the quality of life. The reduced consumption of fat-rich beef, for example, is in part the result of individual efforts to reduce cholesterol intake and the risk of heart disease'.[7]

Adjustments are not only possible but are essential if deepening environmental crisis is to be avoided. *The User's Guide to the Environment* begins with the premise that many of the most serious environmental problems can be ascribed to the affluent society. It looks at the environmental crisis from the viewpoint of the individual citizen, shows how the way we live as individuals causes or contributes to environmental problems, and suggests what we can do to alleviate them. It shows what the consumer can do *now* with existing knowledge and technology, entirely independently, at little or no cost in time or money, and with no major sacrifices.

The first two chapters of the book set the stage. Chapter 1 outlines the development of our attitudes to the environment, of environmental problems and responses, and Chapter 2 assesses the state of the environment today. Chapters 3 and 4 outline specific examples of environmental problems caused by the way we live. Chapters 5 and 6 offer concrete advice on corrective action that can be taken by individuals, either by themselves or through voluntary groups.

It would be simplistic to suggest that the solution to environmental problems lies in changes in individual attitudes alone. On the other hand, expecting government or industry to make all the changes is unrealistic and passes the buck. The way people live is the most fundamental threat to the environment. Removing that threat is the most fundamental solution.

THE USER'S GUIDE TO THE ENVIRONMENT

REFERENCES

1 IUCN, UNEP, WWF (1980) *World Conservation Strategy*. IUCN, Gland
2 Foley, Gerald (1981) *The Energy Question*. Penguin, Harmondsworth
3 IUCN, UNEP, WWF (1980) *op cit*
4 Allen, Robert (1980) *How to Save the World*. Kogan Page, London
5 Myers, Norman (1979) *The Sinking Ark*. Pergamon, Oxford
6 Galbraith, J K (1979) *The Affluent Society*. Penguin, Harmondsworth
7 Brown, Lester (1981) *Building a Sustainable Society*. W W Norton, New York

THE ENVIRONMENT IN HISTORY

1

Environmental problems are nothing new. Conservation was becoming part of government policy in the United States 80 years ago. Coal burning made smog a hazard in thirteenth century London. Plato warned about the effects of the destruction of soils and mountain forests in Greece in 400 BC. And environmental degradation is recorded in the Bible: the book of Genesis relates how the cattle herds of Lot and Abraham became so numerous that 'the land could not support them'. Fighting broke out between the two and their families, and the conflict was only resolved when Lot moved to Sodom and Abraham to the hills of Canaan.

The difference between the environmental problems of the past and present is a matter of degree. The problems have never before been so diverse, so deep-rooted, or so serious. The seeds of today's crisis emerged almost as soon as humans learned to control nature. Old Stone Age man was little more than a hunter-gatherer, limited by lack of skill and strength to living directly off the plant and animal resources of his immediate surroundings. Human impact on the environment was minimal. But this changed as humans invented tools and weapons, migrated and spread, and, with the advantage of experience passed down through generations, learned ordered and seasonally adjusted methods of hunting, of nurturing crops, and of exploiting energy. Although Old Stone Age man was opening up forests to make hunting easier about 250,000 years ago, it was not until the end of the last glaciation of Western Europe 30,000 to 15,000 years ago that organized hunting began to have a lasting impact on the environment. The more advanced and skilful palaeolithic man succeeded in hunting animals such as the sabre-toothed tiger and the mammoth to extinction. Other species were controlled and domesticated.

Mesolithic man (8000 to 3500 BC) may have begun clearing forests because they were the home of threatening wild animals such as bears, wolves and wild cattle. Originally, humans were largely at the mercy of the elements, but subsequently, as they developed, they began to learn about using the environment to their advantage. A key turning point was the first agricultural revolution. In the Fertile Crescent of Asia Minor in about 6000 BC, humans learned that the same piece of land could grow crops more than once if left fallow between seasons of cultivation. The first agricultural surpluses were produced. Nomadic tribes, having learned to cultivate crops and domesticate animals, began to settle. By 2000 BC, human society had begun to be organized into village and town communities, and human population had begun to grow. It then stood at about 100 million. The increasing efficiency of agriculture allowed people to turn their attention to the development of communities, cities and states, and to learn more about how their environment could be used. The Chinese invented the waterwheel and the Arabs the windmill. These increasingly efficient methods of harnessing energy encouraged still further human expansion.

Even at this early stage of human development the environment was being adversely affected. Irrigation in the Mesopotamian plain had begun in 4000 BC. Inefficient drainage led to the soil becoming waterlogged, which, in turn, built up salts in the soil. By 1700 BC, grain yields had been more than halved, and no wheat was being grown in the southern part of the plain. Futile attempts were made in the third century AD to restore irrigation to the area, and even now large parts of the plain are still covered in thick salt crusts.[1] The elm almost completely disappeared from north-west Europe between 3400 and 2800 BC because of the heavy human demand for elms for leaf fodder.[2] This was probably the first major environmental impact on forests made by prehistoric man. Slash and burn agriculture took hold during neolithic times after 3000 BC. Forest clearance led to increased run-off of surface water, erosion and the loss of nutrients in the soil. Intensive grazing and crop cultivation in Britain accelerated the leaching of nutrients from the soil in the uplands, with the result that already by the first century BC much of the upland forest of the British Isles had gone.

However, all was not destruction and careless development. Some of the earliest Western attempts to preserve and study species were also recorded. It was probably concern about the effects of hunting and the spread of cultivation that had encouraged the creation of game reserves and protective laws in Iran before 5000 BC. Tree parks were created in Babylon and Assyria in 1100 BC, and a botanical garden in Nineveh (in present-day Iraq) in 700 BC.[3]

Roman Britain was still heavily covered in woodland (35 per cent cover compared with 9 per cent today), and the Romans did little to alter the British environment beyond starting to reclaim the Fens and other wetlands. It was the Angles and the Saxons who began the systematic clearance of the thick and almost impenetrable forests of the lowlands. The auroch (wild ox) had probably become extinct in Britain during the Bronze Age, but brown bears, wolves, wild boars, beavers, eagles and even vultures probably survived, posing a threat to anyone attempting to clear lowland forest. The bear and the beaver had vanished by the tenth century AD, and the extinction of the boar and wolf followed soon after.

Recent research has revealed that the collapse of the Mayan civilization of central America in AD 900 was caused by soil erosion. Over a period of 1,700 years, the Mayan population had grown, putting increasing pressure on agricultural land. Topsoil was washed into nearby lakes and the cropland drained of its fertility. Over a period of a few decades in the tenth century, the civilization suddenly collapsed, its population reduced to a tenth of its former total.[4]

European man began early to reveal a bias against nature. Roderick Nash argues that, when humans emerged from their primitive state after millions of years of living unprotected in nature, wilderness was seen as negative and hostile, and an inability to control nature was considered a weakness. The Greeks and Romans celebrated nature, but only in its cultivated, pastoral form. The word 'panic' arose from the fear that gripped travellers in the wilderness who thought they heard the approach of Pan, the god of the woods. The Old Testament clearly shows how the Hebrews saw wilderness as cursed. When God was pleased, he transformed wilderness into a land of plenty. When he was displeased, people were banished to the wilderness. Adam and Eve were driven from the Garden of Eden, a paradise where there was nothing to fear and all was provided, into the wilderness. In much early European mythology, such as the eighth century Anglo-Saxon Beowulf, wilderness was the haunt of monsters, trolls, ogres and wild men.[5]

It has been argued that at the root of European attitudes was the Judaeo-

Christian belief that God gave man dominion over the earth, to subdue and turn to his own uses.[6] The attitudes of Judaeo-Christianity contrasted starkly with those of other cultures, which often taught respect for nature and regarded nature as holy, with gods taking the form of animals. A human being was just another animal, sometimes even less privileged than other animals. For Buddhists and Hindus, humans were understood to be a part of nature. Chinese Taoists were inspired by the natural world, and early Chinese progress in agriculture and animal husbandry tended to work with nature rather than against it. Even so, as early as the fourth century BC, the Taoist Chuang Hsu was deploring the end of the age when humanity lived in harmony with nature. The Shinto worshipped nature, seeing gods in mountains, rocks, forests and storms (although this did not prevent the Japanese later developing the most industrialized and heavily pollutive of all societies).

The tribal communities of Africa and North and South America held similar attitudes. The North American Indians had a particular affinity with nature. The Sioux Chief Luther Standing Bear once observed: 'We do not think of the great open plains, the beautiful rolling hills, and the winding streams with tangled growth as "wild". Only to the white man was nature a "wilderness" . . . to us it was tame. Earth was bountiful and we were surrounded with the blessings of the Great Mystery'.[7] Many indigenous peoples still have a far better understanding and appreciation of their environment and how it should be managed than do industrial societies. A project launched in Canada in 1984 recruited the Inuit (Eskimo) people of northern Quebec to use their accumulated knowledge of the area to help draw up a conservation plan.[8] The Indians of South America and South East Asia have pointed out plants with valuable medicinal properties to Western scientists.

Despite the prevailing hostile attitudes to nature in the West, isolated instances of preservation continued throughout the Middle Ages. Infertile land was set aside for game reservation in England by the Saxons and the Normans. As many as two million hectares out of a total of 15 million (five out of 37 million acres) in England and Wales may have been set aside in medieval times as royal forests and hunting grounds, incidentally protecting all other plants and animals within their boundaries. The Inner Farne off the coast of Northumberland may have been managed as a nature reserve by St Cuthbert in the seventh century, and the Abbotsbury Swannery in Dorset has been a nature reserve since

1393. The first enforceable conservation law in England, designed to protect wildfowl eggs, was passed in 1534 by Henry VIII.[9] Centuries of forest clearance – mainly for agriculture – finally moved Elizabethans to voice their concern for supplies of timber, a major raw material in house and ship-building and a major source of energy. In the sixteenth and seventeenth centuries, efforts were made to protect trees, especially oaks, threatened by the demand for charcoal used in iron smelting. The rate of deforestation particularly alarmed the Royal Navy, which relied on timber to build its ships. Tree-planting became a national policy during the late seventeenth century. Several edicts were passed restricting felling and encouraging the management of plantations. Controls were also suggested to prevent polluting industries from being established in London.[10] With all the coal being burned, smog had been a problem in London as early as the thirteenth century.

THE INDUSTRIAL REVOLUTION

The impact of human control over the environment increased markedly from the fifteenth century with the voyages of discovery, which exported the values and knowledge of Western civilization. The growth of trade networks spread the net of environmental exploitation wider, with raw materials and local resources being exported north to meet the growing demands of Europeans. By the end of the eighteenth century, the world population had grown to about 700 million. At this time, population was growing particularly fast in Britain, where demand for food, energy and other resources seemed to be outstripping supply. The smelting of pig-iron depended upon ready supplies of timber. With the little timber that now remained being conserved for ship-building and construction, an alternative method had to be found or iron-making would collapse. In 1709 Abraham Darby found the answer in coke. Thereafter coal became an essential raw material. Thereby, observes Gerald Foley, 'Britain had survived a resource crisis of a kind which had destroyed previous civilisations'.[11] The development of the beam engine and subsequently the rotary engine made possible the more efficient and effective mining of coal, and the industrial revolution escalated.

In the manufacturing industries iron largely replaced wood. The railway era was born. Shipping brought raw materials from all over the world to feed Britain's manufacturing industries. Food and energy became more accessible, and demand for both increased rapidly. Britain's growing power was based firmly on the exploitation of the raw materials and natural resources of its colonies. When Gandhi was asked in 1947 if he would like newly independent India to become like Britain, he replied that British power had been based on the resources of many countries and he would not want India to repeat the process.

There was a second agricultural revolution in Europe during the period 1750 to 1850. To meet the needs of a growing population, new methods of cultivating crops and rearing livestock were developed. In Britain since the fifteenth century, the demand for more profits from farming had led to the enclosure of land previously treated as commons by villagers. This process accelerated rapidly after about 1750. As agriculture became more efficient, so agricultural workers lost their jobs. Between 1700 and 1900 the proportion of people employed in agriculture fell from 80 per cent to 10 per cent. People were drawn to the cities, where the Victorian working class congregated in slums, and the air in cities was fouled by the emissions of large-scale coal burning. The disposal of sewage and refuse were even more serious concerns.

In 1864, the first systematic study of the human impact on the environment was published – Man and Nature by George Perkins Marsh (1801-1885). An American diplomat, Marsh has been cited as the man who invented conservation. He was certainly one of the first to warn that environmental destruction ultimately threatened human existence. His book, which recorded the changes made to the environment by human activity, pointed out the dangers of such changes, and discussed the need for restoration and conservation. Marsh argued that Rome and Greece had inherited fertile land and plentiful resources, but had mismanaged them and that deforestation, soil erosion and the waste of water resources had hastened the fall of the Roman Empire.[12]

In 1876, Friederich Engels wrote that the essential difference between man and other animals was that animals merely used their environment, while man mastered it and made it serve his ends. But, he warned, 'let us not . . . flatter ourselves overmuch on account of our human victories over nature. For each such victory nature takes its revenge on us . . . We are acquiring a better understanding of [the laws of nature] and getting to perceive both the more immediate and the more remote consequences of our interference with the traditional course of nature'.[13]

This growing understanding spawned the organized conservation movement – mainly in Europe and North America – in the nineteenth century.

THE EARLY BRITISH CONSERVATION MOVEMENT

In Britain, conservation developed in several distinct stages, encouraged first by the natural history movement and subsequently by the protectionist and amenity movements.[14] The study of natural history began to flower in the seventeenth and eighteenth centuries.[15] The work of the Swedish naturalist Carolus Linnaeus provided the basis for modern botanical and zoological classification. In 1788, Gilbert White's *The Natural History of Selborne* was published. White, a country vicar, had spent almost all his life in and around the parish of Selborne in Hampshire, compiling field records on the local mammal, bird and plant life. His book had an enormous impact, subsequently earning him the title of father of field natural history. It had a major influence on Darwin. Natural history was given a further boost by the invention of lithography, which brought the visual beauty of nature to a wider audience through the work of men like Thomas Bewick (1753-1828), who helped make natural history one of the most popular pastimes of Victorian society. The word 'ecology' was probably first used in 1873 – possibly earlier.[16] In the nineteenth century, the improvement of transport made the countryside and the study of nature more accessible to an increasing number of people looking for leisure and self-improvement. Most of them wanted to contemplate and study nature rather than preserve or protect it as an end in itself. Natural history and ornithology led to the craze for collecting specimens, and there was a corresponding growth in the damage done to plants and animals. Much collecting was done for bona fide research purposes, but there were many naturalists who vied with each other to build up bigger and better private collections of specimens.

The ravages of collecting and the wanton slaughter and cruelty inflicted by some hunters attracted much condemnation, spawning a protectionist movement. The Society for the Prevention of Cruelty to Animals (later Royal), founded in 1824 to campaign against cruelty to domesticated animals, began turning its attention to wild animals in the middle of the century. By the 1870s it was investigating vivisection, pigeon-shooting, stag-hunting, and rabbit-coursing. Another protectionist society formed at this time was the East Riding Association for the Protection of Sea Birds, which may have been the first wildlife preservation body in the world.[17] It was founded in 1867 to campaign against the annual shoot of seabirds off Flamborough Head in Yorkshire, which had been going on since 1830. Parties of gunmen were taken by steamer to the headland, where they fired indiscriminately at the many seabirds that nested there, using them simply as moving targets.

Cruelty to animals was regarded as an expression of the most savage and primitive side of human nature. Protectionists saw themselves as helping to preserve the fabric of society, and their methods, and those of other popular social reform movements – particularly anti-slavery – began rubbing off on naturalists. One of the first national campaigns was against the use of plumage in women's fashions. The demand for plumage, particularly from gulls, was causing widespread destruction of bird life. Four Acts of Parliament between 1869 and 1880 helped protect local birds, but new supplies were imported from the tropics in the 1880s. In the six months from November 1884 to April 1885, for example, the plumage of more than 770,000 birds was sold on the London market.[18] Those most opposed to the killing of birds for plumage were women themselves – at least those for whom the vogue for plumage had no appeal. One of the societies set up at this time was the (later Royal) Society for the Protection of Birds in 1889. The Indian branch of the SPB was behind one of the earliest pieces of legislation against international trade in wildlife – the 1902 Indian government order banning the export of bird skins and feathers.

From the idea of protecting species grew the concept of protecting habitats. Revulsion at the excesses of industry in the late nineteenth century led people to question 'improvements' made to the countryside, such as draining marshes and controlling vermin, and to express concern at the continuing encroachment of urban land upon the countryside.[19] The work of Victorian natural history societies had revealed clear evidence of the destruction of wildlife and there was a growing rejection of the supposed benefits of industry. The squalor of British cities had made the countryside highly desirable and its value for amenity and recreation led to the creation of groups such as the Commons Preservation Society (now Open Spaces Society) in 1865, which campaigned to save land for amenity. The Society had many successes, but it could not buy land. The need for an organization to acquire and hold land and property in perpetuity for the nation was met in 1893 by the creation of the National Trust, which aimed to protect Britain's cultural and natural heritage from the uniformity imposed by industrial development.

While the national park concept (developed by the Americans in the late nineteenth century) gradually spread elsewhere – notably to Canada (1887), Australia (1895), and New Zealand (1894) – it was not received enthusiastically in Britain. The appearance of the bicycle in the 1890s and the manufacture of inexpensive cars from 1911 made the countryside increasingly accessible, and the National Trust was actively acquiring land for preservation. But the Trust was as much concerned with sites of cultural interest as with nature reserves, inviting some criticism that it acquired land for nature reserves almost randomly with little regard for its national significance. The Society for the Promotion of Nature Reserves (now the Royal Society for Nature Conservation) was founded in 1912 to encourage the Trust to be more discerning. It made a nationwide survey of sites worth protecting and attracted support for their acquisition. But the problem of curbing cruelty to animals was still regarded as more urgent than the setting up of protected areas. The Council for the Protection of Rural England (CPRE) was set up in 1926 to co-ordinate the voluntary conservation movement and campaigned for the creation of national parks. But it was not in fact until after the Second World War that the first British national parks were set up – and they were in reality anything but national, with almost all the land privately owned and still actively farmed.

CONSERVATION IN THE UNITED STATES

For British conservationists at the turn of the century, the challenge was to rescue both wildlife and countryside from the excesses of human activity. In the United States, by contrast, where vast tracts of the West were, for the first time, being opened up by white settlers, the concern was to save nature before it was overrun. There had been isolated instances of conservation on the eastern seaboard during the early years of European settlement: William Penn, for example, when Pennsylvania was founded in the seventeenth century, ruled that settlers should leave an acre of trees for every five acres cleared.[20]

The real boost for American conservation came with the movement westwards in the nineteenth century, which produced two contrasting results. On the one hand, much was destroyed. The herds of buffalo were decimated by gunmen riding trains westwards who picked off buffaloes that dotted the plains. The westward movement brought the new white settlers up against the Indians of the interior, for whom nature had considerable significance and value and whose understanding of human dependence on nature was far in advance of that of the European. In a letter to the President in 1855 regarding the proposed sale of his tribe's land, Chief Seathl (Seattle) of the Suwamish asked 'how can you buy or sell the sky – the warmth of the land? . . . One portion of the land is the same to (the white man) as the next, for he is a stranger who comes in the night and takes from the land whatever he needs. The earth is not his brother, but his enemy, and when he has conquered it, he moves on'.

On the other hand, the discovery of spectacular wilderness areas gave a few people the idea that some land at least was worth preserving for its own sake. And there were some whites who saw the value in saving wilderness. In 1865, an Act of Congress preserved the Yosemite Valley in California for public recreation. In 1872 the world's first national park was created at Yellowstone in Wyoming. The Scottish-born naturalist John Muir spearheaded the preservationist campaign. Muir shunned civilization, went walking alone in the wilderness for weeks at a time, and never shaved in his life. Intensely religious, he regarded his obsession with nature as having made him freer than any man he knew. He campaigned actively to preserve the Sierras of the American West, and was one of the founders in 1892 of the Sierra Club.[21]

While men like Muir spoke of 'protection' and 'preservation', a faction of professional American foresters, hydrologists and geologists had begun promoting 'conservation', or rational management of natural resources. The campaign to conserve forests (for lumber, to protect soils and to ensure an adequate water supply) was led by Gifford Pinchot, a wealthy Pennsylvanian who had studied forestry in Europe and won the support of President Theodore Roosevelt (1901-1909). Pinchot's philosophy was that the conservation movement should have development as its first principle. The United States was the first country to adopt and apply conservation as policy.

Following the campaign to conserve forests came efforts to conserve and manage inland waterways. The importance of rivers in inland transport, domestic and commercial water supply, flood and erosion control and hydroelectric power was advocated by conservationists who saw multi-purpose river development as an example of the planned and efficient use of resources. In 1908, Roosevelt hosted a conference of State governors to discuss conservation of waterways and subsequently of all resources. This succeeded in bringing the word 'conservation' to the attention of the American public for the first time. Roosevelt also hosted the North American Conservation Congress in 1909 (between Canada, Newfoundland, Mexico and the US) and issued invitations for a world conservation congress in The Hague, but his term of office ended before he could take it further.[22]

A classic instance of the differences between preservationists and conservationists was the building of the Hetch Hetchy dam above Yosemite in California. Muir and the preservationists were opposed to any development in the area, while Pinchot and the conservationists regarded the dam as a multi-purpose development which would provide water for San Francisco, control floods and erosion, irrigate crops and generate electricity. After a considerable fight between public sentiment and political ambition, which sapped Muir's energy and hastened his death in 1914, the dam was built.

Conservation in the United States reached a new peak of achievement during the early years of Franklin D Roosevelt's administration (1933-45). It was applied as the cornerstone of economic recovery in Roosevelt's New Era, notably in the Tennessee Valley Authority, the most complete example of a multi-purpose development. Created in 1933, it is now the country's biggest producer of electricity. Roosevelt's Civilian Conservation Corps deployed unemployed men in forestry, soil erosion prevention, flood control and similar projects. And as the United States came out of the Great Depression, visits to national parks soared from 6.3 million in 1934 to 16.2 million in 1938.

Roosevelt himself was unimpressed by most parks, but saw them as essential to the process of moral rejuvenation.

CONSERVATION BECOMES INTERNATIONAL

While national preservation and conservation movements were emerging in most European and North American countries in the first half of the nineteenth century, there was a parallel growth in international contacts which aimed to take a co-ordinated view of the world's common natural problems. Many problems, such as trade in wildlife and the protection of migratory species, required international co-operation. Congresses held during the late nineteenth century resulted in a convention between several European countries in 1902 to protect birds which were useful to agriculture. At the same time, European colonial powers began considering the threats to wildlife in their colonies, which had become popular hunting grounds. A convention aimed at protecting African game animals was signed in 1900 between Britain, Germany, France, Italy, Portugal and the Belgian Congo. In 1903, the Society for the Preservation of the Wild Fauna of the Empire (now the Fauna and Flora Preservation Society) was set up in London, which confirmed the growing concern for wildlife in the colonies. Around 1910, for example, about 150 to 200 shooting parties were visiting British East Africa annually, killing about 10,000 animals. Many of these were the larger mammals: elephants, lions, rhinos, and buffalo.

Concern for the number of animals becoming extinct was now growing: between 1600 and 1900 some 71 bird species and 21 mammal species were known to have become extinct. In fact, the figure may have been much higher; so little was known about wildlife that many species may have been killed off accidentally without being identified. The number of species known to have become extinct, however, was accelerating: there were more species confirmed extinct between 1900 and 1910 (20) than in the whole of the second half of the eighteenth century (17). Most of the extinctions had occurred in tropical regions (for instance, the dodo, the quagga and the blaauwbok), but the Americans had witnessed at first hand one near extinction (the bison) and five bird extinctions.

The most remarkable of these bird extinctions was that of the passenger pigeon, which may once have been the most numerous bird species on earth. Passenger pigeons flew in flocks so large that they darkened the sky and set up winds that created chills over large areas. One flock seen by the naturalist John James Audubon in Kentucky in 1813 took three days to fly past. Another flock was estimated to contain 2,000 million birds. Yet the last passenger pigeon on earth, a female called Martha, died in a zoo in Cincinnati in 1914. The indiscriminate shooting of the birds during the nineteenth century had accounted directly for the death of millions, but the ultimate cause of the extinction of the species is thought to have been indirect. The pigeon was gregarious, and seems to have depended for successful breeding on living in large flocks. Once people began killing passenger pigeons and removing their woodland breeding grounds the species was doomed.[23]

Much of the international activity between the wars rested with the ornithologists, who set up the International Committee for Bird Protection (ICBP) in 1922 to bridge the gap between the growing ornithology movements in Britain and the United States. But concern for the wildlife of Africa in particular was growing. Game hunting continued to be a problem, and was worsened by the extermination of wild animals by colonial authorities who regarded them as agricultural pests or carriers of disease. More than 320,000 animals were killed in anti-tsetse fly operations in Southern Rhodesia between 1924 and 1945 alone.[24] A second international convention was signed in 1933, designed to curb threats to African wildlife by creating protected areas, and superseding the long-defunct 1900 Convention.

On the initiative of a number of Dutch and Swiss preservationists, attempts were made both before and after the First World War to set up a commission for the international protection of nature, but the organizers had little success in whipping up enthusiasm for the idea among national nature protection groups. Critics of the idea felt there were not yet enough established national bodies to merit an international body. Britain and the US, for their part, were interested in some of the issues which affected Africa at the time, but little more. There were, however, conferences on bird protection and international agreements on migratory birds and on nature protection and wildlife preservation in the Western Hemisphere.

THE EMERGENCE OF IUCN

Following the Second World War, a new climate of internationalism emerged in which countries tried to set up the institutions necessary to prevent the misunderstandings which had led to two world wars within three decades. It was only at this time that any real progress was made on the international conservation front. The Swiss and the Dutch revived their attempts to set up an international nature protection body, and in 1948 the International Union for the Protection of Nature (IUPN) was founded.[25] It was supported and encouraged by UNESCO, thanks to the personal interest and involvement of UNESCO's first Director-General, Julian Huxley.

IUPN was essentially the creation of a small group of enthusiastic nature protectionists. It had some good ideas, but almost no money; a combination of financial problems and the absence of many national groups to work with were to stop it from functioning properly throughout the 1950s. IUPN also divorced itself from the emerging UN agencies. It had little to do with the UN Food and Agriculture Organization (FAO), for example, which was already thinking about the question of conserving and managing natural resources to help resolve the world food shortage. FAO planned to promote the protection and extension of forest cover to check soil erosion, protect watersheds, control floods and act as windbreaks and shelter for wildlife.

IUPN missed out on what might have been an ideal opportunity to influence UN thinking when it held its own separate conference on nature protection in 1949, instead of taking part in the simultaneous UN Conference on the Conservation and Utilization of Resources (UNSCCUR), held at Lake Success in New York State. UNSCCUR was a conference well ahead of its time. The issues it discussed – global resources and their interdependence, the development of new resources, and the adequacy of existing resources to meet growing demands – would not be seriously considered again until the late 1960s.[26]

IUPN was too concerned with the limited goal of nature protection to become involved in these wider issues. The Union deemed its first priority was to investigate the degree of the problems facing nature and to decide on corrective action. But the world was too preoccupied with rebuilding economies and societies to be particularly worried about the welfare of wildlife, and IUPN was left to work almost alone. In the 1950s, the enthusiasts who had launched IUPN were gradually replaced by more experienced administrators and scientists who became convinced that the protection of nature for its own sake was not feasible in a world where wildlife had to compete for land with the demands of a rapidly growing human population. A conference on nature protection in Africa, held in Bukavu in the Belgian Congo in 1953, had concluded that creating nature reserves was not in itself the answer to protecting the environment, and that action was needed to conserve vegetative cover, soil, water and other natural resources. In line with the change of emphasis, and on the insistence of some of its US members, IUPN changed its name in 1956 to the International Union for Conservation of Nature and Natural Resources (IUCN). It commissioned ecological surveys of African and Asian countries during the 1950s to assess problems, but had neither the money nor the influence to take effective or co-ordinated action. The need for money to finance IUCN projects was behind the foundation in 1961 of the World Wildlife Fund. Originally seen as a charity that would raise money for IUCN projects, WWF ultimately developed an identity of its own.

Meanwhile, decolonization was under way and nature protectionists in Europe felt it necessary to encourage newly independent countries to pledge their support for the principles of conserving their wildlife and natural resources. In countries such as Kenya, Uganda, Tanzania and Zambia, these resources were, because of tourism, often the main potential source of income. But nature protection was generally seen as a minor issue by the governments of most emerging nations, which had more pressing economic and social needs. There were few teachers, doctors, skilled workers or managers; little money with which to develop resources; inequitable land distribution; and trading systems which favoured – and still do favour – the ex-colonial powers. The priority of most newly independent countries was to develop their economic strength and provide basic social services for their people. With development their priority, they regarded conservation as of minor importance. Yet uncontrolled and unplanned development, where little or no heed was paid to the impact of development on the environment, was the very thing most likely in the long term to undermine rather than strengthen economies.

THE LIMITS TO GROWTH

The industrialized countries of the North* had just emerged from a phase of concerted national economic recovery after the ravages of the Second World War, and had entered an economic boom. The 'consumer' society was born, consuming food, energy (especially oil and coal), household goods and appliances. Miles of new roads were built to cope with increased traffic, together with new power stations and factories. All this created accelerating problems of waste. Ironically, affluence also gave people the leisure and time to think about social

*The terms 'North' and 'South' are used respectively to describe the industrialized countries of Europe, North America, the Soviet bloc and Japan, and the countries of Africa, Asia and Latin America. The distinction, which is based largely on economic factors, is guilty of generalization and may well be misleading. But there are enough environmental problems common to the countries in each group to excuse the distinction.

problems, and there was a generally increased awareness of issues such as nuclear disarmament, racism and the environment. With the quality of their lives improving, people became less tolerant of the more visible aspects of environmental degradation, especially pollution.

A classic example was the concern over London smogs, caused by the build-up of sulphur dioxide from the burning of coal fires. About 4,000 people died and tens of thousands became ill from heart and lung disorders as a result of the smog of 1952 alone. Smog had been a problem in London on and off since the thirteenth century. The smogs of Victorian London were infamous, and lent a dramatic air to the exploits of Sherlock Holmes. Londoners had long known their city as the Old Smoke. Following the 1952 smog, however, government response was rapid. In 1954, a Clean Air Bill was introduced; in 1955 London was declared a smokeless zone; and in 1956 the Clean Air Act was passed, controlling smoke emissions. The effects of decades of city smoke are currently being washed off as London's buildings are cleaned and restored. The Houses of Parliament now look nearly as the architects Barry and Pugin intended for the first time since the mid-nineteenth century.

Until the 1960s, active concern for the environment had been expressed almost wholly in terms of the protection of nature and wildlife. At this point came the realization that the threats posed to wildlife were just one aspect of a much wider catalogue of damage and deterioration brought on by human activity. In 1962, Rachel Carson's *Silent Spring* was published, graphically illustrating the effects of the misuse of synthetic pesticides and insecticides. The book had a major impact on public thinking, particularly in the United States. It helped to convince people that pollution not only offended eyes and noses, but could actually undermine life itself.[27] Pollution – the problem of affluence producing effluent – became the first popular environmental issue of the 1960s, followed closely by debates over the effects of population growth, which many believed was the root cause of all other environmental problems. The environment became an increasingly popular activist cause. In the United States it rivalled the civil rights and anti-war campaigns in popular interest. It was fuelled by the growing chorus of arguments that humanity was stepping outside the limits of the earth to sustain and support population growth, resource consumption, and economic, industrial and agricultural growth.

A succession of environmental disasters gave considerable publicity to the issues, and generated more support. In 1966 a coal slag heap poised above the Welsh mining village of Aberfan collapsed, killing 144 people, 116 of them children in the local school. In 1967, the oil tanker Torrey Canyon spilled 875,000 barrels of oil into the English Channel, and this was followed two years later by a 77,000-barrel blow-out off Santa Barbara, California. There have been far greater disasters since (the 1979-80 blow-out of the Mexican Ixtoc I well involved 3.1 million barrels of oil), but Torrey Canyon and Santa Barbara were the first in a long line of such incidents, and as such had maximum effect. The Santa Barbara spill convinced Americans that the protection of the environment would not simply happen, but that it needed active public support and involvement.

The human effects of environmental pollution were illustrated by the Minamata tragedy in Japan. Chemical production had begun on the shores of Minamata Bay (opposite Nagasaki) as early as 1939, and mercury wastes dumped into the bay. In 1953, it was noticed that birds and cats in the area were behaving strangely. By 1956, neurological disorders were being found among fishing families. The chemical company denied any relationship between its dumping and 'Minamata disease' as it became known, but nevertheless, by the early 1960s, the company had begun paying small amounts of compensation to disease victims. When the residents of another village, Niigata, successfully won a civil action against a factory polluting the waters there, the courts ruled in favour of the Minamata victims and they were compensated in 1973. There was another case in Mitsui, where a factory had been pouring untreated cadmium, zinc and lead wastes into a local river, and at Yokkaichi, where air pollution from a petro-chemical complex had caused respiratory diseases locally. By 1971, more than 450 local anti-pollution campaigns had sprung up in Japan. Pollution in Tokyo Bay was said to be so severe that a film could be developed in water from the bay. Japan's problems seemed to confirm the negative side-effects of unbridled industrial growth.

Incidents such as Torrey Canyon and Minamata, and the findings of ecologists, scientists and planners studying patterns of resource consumption and population growth caused a growing sense of alarm and the prediction of real and imaginary disasters. Many of the effects were later found to have been exaggerated. For example, it was predicted in 1971 that up to 500 supersonic airliners (SSTs) would take to the air during the 1970s and that, by 1985, a fleet of 300 Concordes, together with an expanded Boeing fleet, would be using up oil equivalent to one-ninth of the world's total 1971 demand.[28] In 1972 it was predicted that by 1985 all land surfaces other than the coldest and highest would be occupied and utilized by man.[29] Events have proved both predictions very wrong.

The early flights of Apollo spacecraft in the mid-1960s produced the first photos of the earth floating free in space, graphically emphasizing the concept of Spaceship Earth that emerged in 1965: the idea of the earth as a spaceship on which humanity travelled dependent on its vulnerable and limited supplies of air and soil.[30] A bevy of environmental gurus and philosophers emerged, most of them American and many branded 'prophets of doom' because of their predictions of disaster for the earth if people continued to live as wastefully as they had been. Ralph Nader spearheaded the crusade against pollution in the United States, arguing that it was a political issue that could not be tackled by the traditional conservation movement because it was not sufficiently politicized. Barry Commoner, a biology professor, argued that the environmental crisis was not a result of affluence or over-population, but of growth in the use of technologically harmful products. He was one of the leading activists who campaigned against nuclear testing. Another biology professor, Paul Ehrlich of Stanford University, felt that the preoccupation with pollution was missing the point and that every environmental problem ultimately stemmed from over-population. His book *The Population Bomb* was published in 1967 and became the best selling environmental book ever, with three million copies in paperback published by the mid-1970s. He was writing when the world population was 3.5 billion. Today (1985) it is over 4.5 billion and still climbing rapidly.

One of the most controversial prophets of doom was yet another biology professor, Garret Hardin, who coined the phrase 'tragedy of the commons'. He used the parable of a commons on which several herders grazed their cattle. The cattle ate grass at the same rate as it grew — supply and demand were in perfect balance. Then one herder decided that he could add one more cow and reap the benefits while the cost was shared among the other herders, whose cows would have to settle for less. The herder's argument was that if he did not do it, the others would, and he would then have to go without. But what if every herder reached the same conclusion at the same time? Hardin felt everyone was locked into a system where each felt compelled to increase his or her demands of a world where supplies were strictly limited. He rejected appealing to people's consciences, claiming that they would have to be forced to control themselves, especially as regards reproduction.[31]

Following hot on the heels of the gurus came the reports. *The Ecologist*'s 'A Blueprint for Survival' (1970)[32] and the Club of Rome's 'The Limits to Growth' (1972)[33] warned of the limits to the earth's capacity to support human demands. More and more people began to realize that life on earth was a huge and interrelated ecological system, that the earth's resources were not in infinite supply, that consumerism was leading to widespread destruction and degradation of resources, and that there were limits to the demands the earth could tolerate. The hippies of the 1960s spearheaded the anti-establishment movement that rejected the obsession with success and security of older generations. Materialism, technology, power, profit and growth were seen as symbols of all that was bad, and which posed the greatest threat to the environment.

The popular environmental movement reached its peak during the late 1960s and 1970s. Earth Day – 22 April 1970 – attracted thousands of people to more than 11,500 gatherings across the United States. In its wake it left a large number of people convinced of the need for change. One of the legacies was the birth of campaigning pressure groups. The Sierra Club, one of America's oldest – and today most effective – conservation groups, still clung in the 1960s to many of the preservationist principles of its founder John Muir. Its charismatic executive director, David Brower, set out to haul it into the forefront of environmental activism and threw its resources into opposing projects such as the plan to build two dams in the Grand Canyon. Brower placed newspaper advertisements with headlines like 'Should we also flood the Sistine Chapel so the tourists can get nearer the ceiling?', and mobilized the Sierra Club, increasing the membership ten-fold in the process. But the Club's charitable status was taken away, and the board of directors accused Brower of abusing his position. Brower was removed from office in 1969. He replied by founding Friends of the Earth, set up to campaign actively for the environment and promote more rational use of natural resources. The Sierra Club soon saw which way the wind was blowing and also moved actively into campaigning. Brower is now back on the board of directors of the Club while Friends of the Earth has gone on to mobilize public support for environmental campaigns in 28 countries.

Within months of the launch of Friends of the Earth, a group of North American protesters called the Don't Make a Wave Committee had sailed a small boat into the vicinity of an American nuclear test in the Aleutian islands. The tests were postponed, so the same tactics were applied to French tests in the Muroroa Atoll in 1972 and 1973. The Committee had by then become Greenpeace, and when the French detonated a bomb with a Greenpeace vessel only 20km away, considerable publicity was attracted for the environmental cause. Greenpeace went on to campaign against whaling, sealing, nuclear power and radioactive waste disposal, all the time setting up events and stunts that attracted maximum publicity to the issue.

Not only were young people involved in these campaigns: political parties had begun to see the expediency of adopting policies on the environment and of being seen to be taking action. The period 1969-72 saw a flurry of government activity, with varying success, devoted to the creation of official environmental agencies and the passage of legislation – in the United States, the UK, France, Japan, the USSR, Australia, Canada, West Germany, India, Kenya, Sweden, Switzerland and other countries. International conventions were agreed, notably those dealing with wetlands (1971), the world's cultural and natural heritage (1972), international trade in endangered species (1973) and the conservation of migratory species (1979). There were several treaties on marine oil pollution and its effects. Increased pressure to adopt policies on the environment was placed on member countries by international organizations such as the UN agencies, the European Community, the Council of Europe (which declared 1970 European Conservation Year), and the Organization for Economic Co-operation and Development.

STOCKHOLM AND AFTER

The growing popular and political pressures and interest of the 1960s clearly underlined the degree of interest in the environment and measures to use it more rationally and sustainably. Popular feeling was backed up by the findings of several scientific programmes (such as the International Biological Programme and the Global Atmospheric Research Programme), set up to find out more about the ecological structure of the environment. Surprisingly little was really known. The shift from narrow concerns related to the threats faced by nature and wildlife to a wider interest in the environment as a whole was confirmed in 1972 with the UN Conference on the Human Environment in Stockholm, the watershed event in the development of the environmental movement.

The immediate spur for Stockholm was pollution. Swedish research during the late 1960s confirmed a disturbing increase in the acidity of rain falling in Sweden. The blame was found to lie with emissions from power stations and motor vehicles in Europe's centres of industry – the burning of fossil fuels such as coal, oil and petrol was emitting sulphur and nitrogen oxides into the atmosphere that were reacting with atmospheric vapour to produce rain that was unusually acidic. The Swedes lobbied for a conference to discuss the issue and ways of solving it through international action. The UN eventually agreed to host a conference to discuss the total human environment.

One notable feature of the conference, held in June 1972, was that it had been requested by the North in response to problems that were largely related to industrial societies and of little concern to countries in the South. One of the major stumbling blocks of the conference was the concern felt by the South that any environmental safeguards or restrictions imposed by the North would retard the process of development, and that the North would impose trade restrictions to prohibit, for example, the import of food contaminated by pesticides. Pollution was barely – as yet – a problem in the South.

The major theme to emerge from the conference was the link between the environment and development. Until then, development was seen as the bugbear of environmentalism: it was industrial and agricultural development that was at the root of all environmental problems, and, as such, development and environment were thought to be incompatible. The principle of sustainable development – development that builds on rather than degrades the ecological structure of the environment – had been raised as early as the turn of the century in the United States, again by some UN agencies after the Second World War, and had been discussed increasingly by nature preservationists. Stockholm succeeded in bringing the discussion to a much wider audience, and it was now widely acknowledged that development and environment were mutually supportive. There had to be development but, if it was carefully planned and managed to take account of the ecological characteristics of nature and natural resources, it could be considerably more productive.

What made Stockholm different from all that had gone before was the emphasis on the *human* environment. Most conservation groups had until then concentrated on the protection and management of the natural environment as seen from the perspective of its degradation by humans, and also as something removed from humanity. Only in a few countries, notably the United States, had conservation involved using resources and at the same time managing them carefully. There was now a growing realization that the natural environment could not realistically be managed without considering human needs, particularly in the South, which was richest in natural resources but poorest in economic and technological resources. People in the North began to realize that humans were a part of the environment, not detached from it. In a sense, it was the beginning of a return to the pre-industrial age when people were more conscious of their direct reliance on the environment.

The Stockholm conference produced a series of recommendations and underlined the need for an ordered system of evaluating and reviewing the state of the global environment and for a means of exchanging information and knowledge. The most tangible result of the conference was the creation of the United Nations Environment Programme (UNEP), designed to be the environmental 'conscience' of the UN system and to guide and co-ordinate environmental programmes among the other UN bodies. UNEP has since experienced mixed fortunes. It has had no real powers to interfere in the affairs of countries or other UN bodies; it has suffered the usual problems of the UN bureaucratic structure; it has too little money to do all it should; and it is torn between the interests of the North and the South. On the other hand, the organization has helped promote international environmental co-operation (especially in tackling the problems of pollution in regional seas such as the Mediterranean and the Red Sea); it has promoted the establishment of environmental monitoring systems within other UN bodies; it has helped encourage the overseas assistance agencies of the North to pay heed to environmental questions when planning or funding development projects in the South; and has generally helped raise awareness of the environmental problems that affect the international community.

Awareness of the problems, and some of the solutions, has grown rapidly since Stockholm, aided by a series of influential UN conferences on population, human settlements, new and renewable energy, desertification, food, water and climate. Understanding of the links between human activity and environmental degradation is growing daily. But this is not reflected in success in solving the problems. Just before her death in 1981, Barbara Ward, the British economist and author, observed that 'for an increasing number of environmental issues the difficulty is not to identify the remedy, because the remedy is now well understood. The problems are rooted in the society and the economy – and in the end in the political structure'.[34] The case of desertification illustrates this point.

In 1977, the UN sponsored a Conference on Desertification aimed at drawing attention to the increasingly urgent issue of the global spread of desert conditions. The need for action had been emphasized by the 1968-73 Sahelian drought, in which between 100,000 and 250,000 people and up to 3.5 million head of cattle had died. About one-third of the earth's land surface is naturally desert or semi-desert, but increasing demands from both humans and livestock has encouraged the spread of desert conditions. In 1977, about 600 to 700 million people were thought to face the risk of the consequences of desertification. The Plan of Action that came out of the conference recommended action needed to halt desertification. Seven years later, at a two-day meeting in May 1984, UNEP admitted that the goal of halting desertification by the turn of the century was unrealistic. Despite the fact that people knew what corrective action was needed, almost nothing had been done. Very little money had been raised to finance anti-desertification projects. The South was giving a low priority to fighting desertification and governments were taking too little interest in the implications.[35]

The hazards posed by the storage, transport and disposal of toxic wastes has seen some public interest and government action, thanks in no small measure to the power of the issue to make the headlines. The number of storage sites for hazardous wastes has increased in recent years, and now runs into thousands. The dangers were graphically highlighted in the late 1970s by events at Love Canal. An uncompleted, abandoned nineteenth century waterway near Niagara Falls in New York State, Love Canal had been used as an industrial dump since the 1930s. In 1953 it was filled in, and homes, a school and a playing field were built on and around the site. In 1976, following heavy rain and snow, chemicals began seeping into the basements of the homes. The abnormal incidence of miscarriages, birth defects, cancer and other illnesses led in 1978 to the declaration of the site as a disaster area, and by July 1979 some 263 families had been evacuated and 1,000 more advised to leave their homes.[36]

During the 1960s, nuclear power was hailed as the great new source of energy for the future. In 1970, it was predicted that it would account for half the energy generating capacity of North America, Europe and Japan by 1985. There were predictions of 100 nuclear power stations being built every year in the 1980s, many of them in the South. But nuclear power now provides only a fraction of the amount of energy once predicted. In 1983, there were just 282 commercial plants in 25 countries – the US, Britain, the USSR, France and Japan accounted for 201 of these. Fears about the safety of reactors, the problems of radioactive waste disposal, and the opportunity that nuclear power stations gave countries to produce nuclear weapons have combined to make nuclear power one of the most contentious issues of the past decade. And nuclear power is no longer as economically competitive as it was once thought to be.[37]

The anti-nuclear power cause was given a boost in March 1979 by an incident at the Three Mile Island nuclear power station in Harrisburg, Pennsylvania. An initial mechanical failure, followed by the failure of a number of back-up systems, and made worse by pumps having been closed down in violation of regulations and slow operator response, caused a shutdown of the reactor. The presence of a large and potentially explosive bubble of radioactive gas in the top of the reactor led to evacuation of the area until the bubble had dissolved into the coolant water. Five other nuclear plants with similar designs were shut down to determine whether they could withstand earthquakes. A demonstration against nuclear power in Washington in May, involving 75,000 people, was the largest anti-nuclear power demonstration ever held, and Three Mile Island became a catch phrase for the anti-nuclear power movement.[38]

The debate about the links between environment and development came to a head in 1980 with the publication of three major reports. The first was the World Conservation Strategy, sponsored by IUCN, UNEP and WWF, which aimed to set out a rational and coherent policy for world conservation. The priorities it listed were to maintain essential life-supporting ecological systems (such as soil and water), to preserve the genetic diversity of the earth's animal and plant species, and to ensure that species and ecosystems were used sustainably. The Strategy argued that development and the environment were not incompatible but were mutually supportive, that one depended on the other. The Strategy also encouraged countries to draw up their own national conservation strategies based on the same principles.[39] Britain was one of the first to respond and published a response in 1983.[40]

The second key report was the Global 2000 report to President Carter, a three-year study commissioned in 1977 and prepared by the US Council on Environmental Quality and the Department of State. It was designed to provide the United States with information on changes in population, natural resources and the environment to the year 2000. The object was to provide an input into longer term planning, but Carter lost office in 1980 and the Reagan administration ignored Global 2000. The main conclusion of the report was summed up in its opening paragraph: 'If present trends continue, the world in 2000 will be more crowded, more polluted, less stable ecologically, and more vulnerable to disruption than the world we live in now. Serious stresses involving population, resources, and environment are clearly visible ahead. Despite greater material output, the world's people will be poorer in many ways than they are today'.[41]

The third major report was that of the Brandt Commission, which argued that major changes were needed in North-South relations, and that many international problems were based on the lack of understanding of the mutual interests between the two sides. One of the Commission's conclusions was that 'the bulk of the depletion of non-renewable resources and the pressure on the oceans and the atmosphere have been caused by the spectacular industrial growth of the developed countries where only one-fifth of the world's people live. But population growth in some parts of the Third World is already a source of alarming ecological change, and its industrialization is bound to lead to greater pressure on resources and the environment'.[42]

Despite the progress made in conserving and managing natural resources, and the attention drawn to the implications of poor environmental management, not everyone is yet convinced of the merits of conservation. The country that has had the longest and most active environmental movement – the United States – has shown how policies can be reversed or abandoned overnight. Until his dismissal in 1983, James Watt was Ronald Reagan's Secretary of State for the Interior, charged with responsibility for 220 million hectares (550 million acres) of federal land and much of US environmental policy. A born-again Christian, he believed implicitly in the teaching of Genesis that God had given man dominion over the earth, and set out to open America's natural resources to the exploiters. He slashed funding for environmental programmes, cut the staff of the relevant government departments, planned to open millions of hectares of Alaskan highlands to oil and gas interests, and described environmentalists as left-wing political activists. In all this he was largely unopposed by President Reagan who, when presented with a million-signature petition demanding Watt's removal, described Watt as his 'favourite' cabinet member. It was President Reagan himself who cut the US contribution to UNEP by 29 per cent, barely pausing for breath before preparing a statement for IUCN in which he spoke of the 'considerable advantages' of conserving resources such as wildlife and the increasing importance of international co-operation in the field of conservation. Ironically, the US environmental movement had previously been going through a trough. Following the challenge thrown down by President Reagan, however, it launched itself into the fray with renewed vigour and motivation.

The environmental movement has gone through a metamorphosis in recent years. Twenty years ago, people knew there was 'a problem' and could see some of the symptoms. Today, much more is understood about the causes of the problem, many more symptoms have been identified, and many of the remedies are seen and understood. But, to borrow a phrase from Winston Churchill, this is only the end of the beginning. Knowing is one thing; doing is another.

REFERENCES

1 Earthscan (1984) *Cropland or wasteland: The problems and promises of irrigation*. Earthscan Press Briefing Document No 38, London

2 Sheail, John (1983) The historical perspective. In Warren, A and Goldsmith, F B (eds) *Conservation in Perspective*. John Wiley, London

3 Nicholson, Max (1970) *The Environmental Revolution*. Hodder and Stoughton, London

4 Deevey, E S *et al* (1979) Mayan urbanism: Impact on a tropical karst environment. In *Science*, 19 October

5 Nash, Roderick (1973) *Wilderness and the American Mind*. Yale University Press, New Haven

6 White, Lynn (1967) The historical roots of our ecological crisis. In *Science*, Vol 155, 10 March

7 McLuhan, T C (ed) (1980) *Touch the Earth*. Abacus, London

8 World Wildlife Fund (1984) *WWF Monthly Report* May

9 Nicholson, Max (1970) *op cit*

10 Ibid

11 Foley, Gerald (1976) *The Energy Question*. Penguin, Harmondsworth

12 Marsh, G P (1974) *Man and Nature*. Harvard University Press, Cambridge, Mass

13 Engels, F (1976) *Dialectics of Nature*. Progress Publishers, Moscow

14 Lowe, Philip and Goyder, Jane (1983) *Environmental Groups in Politics*. George Allen and Unwin, London

15 Allen, David Elliston (1978) *The Naturalist in Britain*. Penguin, Harmondsworth

16 Ibid

17 Lowe, Philip (1983) Values and institutions in British nature conservation. In Warren and Goldsmith *op cit*

18 Sheail, John (1976) *Nature in Trust*. Blackie, Glasgow

19 Lowe and Goyder (1983) *op cit*

20 Huth, Hans (1957) *Nature and the American*. University of Nebraska Press

21 Fox, Stephen (1981) *John Muir and his Legacy*. Little, Brown and Co, Boston

22 Ibid

23 Halliday, Tim (1980) *Vanishing Birds*. Penguin, Harmondsworth

24 Boardman, Robert (1980) *International Organization and the Conservation of Nature*. Macmillan, London

25 Ibid

26 McCormick, John (1985) *The International Environmental Movement: 1945-1980*. Unpublished M.Phil thesis, University of London

27 Carson, Rachel (1971) *Silent Spring*. Penguin, Harmondsworth

28 Inglis, Barclay (1971) Concorde: The case against supersonic transport. In Barr, J (ed) *The Environmental Handbook*. Ballantine, London

29 Ward, B and Dubos, R (1980) *Only One Earth*. Penguin, Harmondsworth

30 Stevenson, Adlai (1965). Speech before UN Economic and Social Council, Geneva

31 Hardin, Garrett (1968) The tragedy of the commons. In *Science*, Vol 162, 13 December

32 A blueprint for survival (1972). In *The Ecologist*, Vol 2, No 1

33 Meadows, D H, Meadows, D L, Randers, J and Behrens, W W (1974) *The Limits to Growth*. Signet, New York

34 Ward, Barbara (1982). In Eckholm, Erik *Down to Earth*. Pluto Press, London

35 Grainger, Alan (1982) *Desertification*. Earthscan, London

36 Council on Environmental Quality (1979) *Environmental Quality 1979*. CEQ, Washington

37 Brown, Lester *et al* (1984) *State of the World 1984*. W W Norton, New York

38 Council on Environmental Quality (1979) *op cit*

39 IUCN, UNEP and WWF (1980) *World Conservation Strategy*. IUCN, Gland

40 UKWCS (1983) *The Conservation and Development Programme for the UK: A Response to the World Conservation Strategy*. Kogan Page, London

41 *The Global 2000 Report to the President* (1982). Penguin, Harmondsworth

42 Independent Commission on International Development Issues (1980) *North-South: A Programme for Survival*. Pan, London

THE STATE OF THE ENVIRONMENT

2

Most environmental problems stem from the wrong kind of development. In the North it tends to be the fault of over-development: too many cars on the road, too much urban spread, too much waste and over-consumption. In the South it tends to be the fault of under-development or of badly planned development: poor land management, clearance of forests for firewood and uncontrolled population growth.

Until recently, not enough has been understood about the effects of development. It is no good building a dam if upriver areas are so badly eroded that the dam will fill with silt. Without adequate drainage, an irrigation system may become waterlogged and useless. A factory built without adequate safeguards can discharge toxic chemicals into rivers and coastal waters, thereby destroying fisheries, and polluting water supply.

Enough people have been concerned about the environment for long enough to suggest that some progress must have been made towards solving the problems. There have been successes it is true. Some pollution has been controlled; some natural land has been preserved; and more materials are being recycled. But it is not yet time to rest on any laurels. Many of these successes have been achieved because both developers and governments have understood the problems, and have seen that it is in their short-term interests to take action. But relatively little is yet known about either the state of the environment or all the long-term effects of human activity.

POPULATION

Because population growth is exponential, it has been only relatively recently that the world's population has exploded. In 1830, there were one billion people on earth. It took only one hundred years for that figure to double, and just 45 years for it to double again to four billion.

The current total is about 4.5 billion. The predictions are that there will be six billion people by the year 2000. Three out of every four people live in the South, and nearly half the population of Africa and more than one-third of that of Asia and Latin America are under 15 years old. By comparison, only one in four Europeans is under 15, and, because people in the North are living longer, the proportion of people aged 65 and over is greater than ever before.

The English clergyman and economist Thomas Malthus warned as early as the late eighteenth century that, unless population growth was checked, the problems of subsistence would impose their own checks. In 1968, Paul Ehrlich's book *The Population Bomb* described the alarming increase in human population growth, and gave its title to a graphic new catch phrase used to describe the magnitude of the problem. But it was not until the 1970s that the links between population, resources and environment were spelt out clearly. The 1974 UN World Population Conference in Bucharest brought the issues to a head. The more people that have to be fed, housed, clothed, educated, nursed and transported, the more resources are needed, and the more the environment is affected.

In contrast to the talk at Bucharest, and before, of a world not being able to cope with its growing population, the second UN Population Conference in Mexico City in August 1984 seemed to suggest that the world population crisis was over. Although individual countries will continue to face problems, it is now generally agreed that world population growth is slowing to the point where it will stabilize at about ten billion by the end of the next century. But a hundred years is a long time in demography. Many governments are going to continue to suffer the problems described by Erik Eckholm: having their efforts to increase savings for investment, to reduce unemployment, to provide universal education, to protect natural resources and to reduce food imports undermined by surging human numbers.[1] Countries of the South are improving their food production rates faster than most developed countries, but when this is set against population growth, their per capita output is right down; while the North had a steady gain in per capita output of 1.4 per cent between 1961-76, there was less than 1 per cent gain in Africa and Asia, and almost no gain at all during periods of drought. Up to half the children in the South are undernourished; as many as ten million die every year as a result.

The population growth rate for the world as a whole is slowing – from 2 per cent per annum in the 1960s to 1.7 per cent today – but this is hardly reassuring when, at this rate, one million people are born every five days. In 1970, the world population grew by 70 million; in 1983 it grew by 79 million. There are also major regional variations. In Europe the growth rate is 0.4 per cent, and 12 European countries – including the UK – have achieved zero growth rates. In Africa, by contrast, the population is growing at an average of 2.9 per cent annually, faster than any other region. A combination of population growth, inadequate land management and drought has made famine an increasingly characteristic feature of African life. Kenya recently became the first country ever to achieve a population growth rate of more than 4 per cent. At this rate its population will double in 18 years. (In contrast, at its present growth rate it would take nearly 700 years for the population of the EEC to double.) On the whole, better health, education and employment opportunities usually result in a decline in fertility rates. Kenya is one notable exception to this rule.

Almost all countries now have some sort of family planning programme. But simply having a family planning programme does not mean to say that it works. The traditional desire for large families as a form of economic security against infant mortality and old age has not waned. The World Fertility Survey of the 1970s revealed a considerable demand for birth control, much of it unmet because of social pressures to have children, lack of access to contraceptives and lack of knowledge and means. A UN survey in 15 African and Asian countries found that at least one in five women with two children in these countries (which included Bangladesh, Sri Lanka and Korea) wanted no more children. Abortion is still not legally available to one woman in three anywhere in the world. Many family planning programmes fruitlessly try to address themselves to women in societies dominated by men.

But there have been successes. China, with a population of over one billion, has imposed controversial draconian measures to limit families to one child only. It has already cut its growth rate from 2 per cent to 1.2 per cent in a decade, and may well succeed in stabilizing its population by the turn of the century. China may one day be a land with no uncles, aunts, brothers or sisters. India is another country that has had a population policy since 1952 and, although its growth rate is now less than Bangladesh or Pakistan, the results have not been as good as were once expected, so there have recently been renewed attempts to reduce the rate further.

Environmentalists are divided over the role of population in resource problems. While the 1980 World Conservation Strategy made almost no mention of the population factor, many people have been arguing since the 1960s that there can be no progress in environmental planning until population growth rates are cut. But the problem is not the *size* of the world's population; in theory at least, the earth could support many more people than at present. The problem is partly that most countries cannot afford more people, and partly that our present way of life is wasteful of resources, so more people also means more waste, more land degradation, more pollution, less room for other species, and a deteriorating environment.

THE LAND

Land is the most fundamental natural resource, and agriculture the most fundamental economic activity. Over the past 4,000 to 5,000 years, humans have exploited the land by ploughing and planting fields, irrigating pastures, grazing livestock, damming rivers, and building roads, towns and cities. Agriculture, the oldest human activity, now occupies nearly 10 per cent of the earth's land surface. Global 2000 optimistically estimated that a 90 per cent increase in food production could be achieved by using only 2.5 per cent more land than was cultivated in 1978. But soil erosion, agricultural mismanagement, and urban development have so far combined to undermine attempts to increase agricultural output. Up to 15 million hectares (37 million acres) of land, an area half the size of Italy, is thought to be degraded every year. Some of this loss is offset by the reclamation and conversion of new land, but if these losses continue, then, instead of an increase in cropland, there will be a reduction of at best nearly 2 per cent, and at worst 9 per cent, by the end of the century.

Rising demand for land and food is the crucial factor. Helped by new technology, farm output since the Second World War has grown rapidly throughout the world. Between 1950 and 1983, world grain output alone increased by 150 per cent. But demand is exceeding supply: FAO estimates that food, fish and forest production will need to increase by 60 per cent by the end of the century to keep pace with population growth. To make matters worse, there has been a net decline in per capita food production in many parts of the world. In Africa, agricultural production grew by 14 per cent in 1970-79, but population grew by 32 per cent, so the net food output actually fell. Famines have occurred throughout human history, but never on the same scale as at the present time. An estimated 400 to 500 million people are currently undernourished. The drought that struck much of Africa south of the Sahara during 1984 – with particularly tragic consequences in Ethiopia – underlined the potential for a famine of huge proportions in the area. Predictions are that the world demand for grain will double by the end of the century – but per capita output is decreasing.

Agriculture

Agriculture is being widely mismanaged. In the South, the daily quest for survival of peasant farmers living from hand to mouth compels them to settle on marginal land unsuitable for agriculture. Hillsides are cleared of forest cover, land is over-grazed and over-cultivated, and irrigation systems are neglected or mismanaged. With fertile land increasingly hard to find, fertilizers and pesticides (many of them chemical-based) have been used increasingly to stimulate the productivity of existing farmland. Negative effects are already being felt where phosphates and nitrates are washed off the land by rainwater and into rivers and lakes. This causes eutrophication (the proliferation and decay of algae which 'strangles' a river or lake and makes it unfit for fish life) and contaminates drinking water. Pesticides affect wildlife, remain as residues in food (the effects on the health of people eating food sprayed with pesticides is still unclear), and poison the farmworkers who apply it to the land. Oxfam estimates that 375,000 people are poisoned every year in the Third World by pesticides – and 10,000 of them die. While persistent pesticides like DDT have been banned in the North, their cheapness and short-term effectiveness makes them attractive in the South, where they make up half the pesticides in use.

The use of pesticides is a particularly serious problem in irrigated areas, where the lushness of the vegetation, the existence of standing water, and the humid microclimate created by irrigation provide a haven for pests. The increased use of pesticides also has two worrying side-effects: the growing resistance of pests to the chemicals used to kill them, and the decimation of the predatory species that previously fed off the pests.

Irrigated farmland, which accounts for only 15 per cent of the world's total farmland but produces more than 40 per cent of agricultural output, is under threat from mismanagement on every continent. Poor drainage can cause the soil to waterlog or saturate, and this in turn can cause the build-up of salts in the soil, ruining productive land. Salinization now affects more than half the world's irrigated land, and has made wasteland out of 25 million hectares (62 million acres) of once fertile, productive land. In the most heavily irrigated areas, such as the southern Great Plains of the United States, the pumping of water from underground aquifers to irrigate farmland causes groundwater levels to decline. In some parts of California the land has actually subsided.[2]

In the North, intensive agriculture leaves less and less room for wildlife. British farmers are among the most productive in the world... but at what cost? Farming in Britain is so capital- and energy-intensive that the use of chemical fertilizers and pesticides has increased dramatically in the last three decades. The quest for ever greater efficiency encourages farmers to create larger fields by removing hedgerows, traditionally the last haven for nature in seas of man-managed land. Britain's characteristic landscape of fields and hedgerows is giving way to featureless prairie.

Erosion

Erosion, a natural process made far worse by human activity, is stripping millions of tons of fertile soil from the land. More than half of India, for example, suffers some form of soil degradation. So much soil has been washed into the Ganges from the deforested uplands of the Indian subcontinent that a new island has been formed out of silt in the Bay of Bengal, leading to conflict between India and Pakistan over its possession. Wind erosion in northern China is now so serious that scientists at the Mauna Loa observatory in Hawaii can tell when spring ploughing begins in the region by the clouds of dust in the atmosphere.[3] Even in the United States, which suffered the worst effects of bad land management in the dustbowl years of the 1930s, erosion is bad enough to reduce long-term productivity on one in every three hectares. The US Soil Conservation Office considers annual soil losses of 12 tonnes per hectare (5 tons per acre) in deep soils the most that can be tolerated without harming productivity; a recent survey of farms in the Midwest and Great Plains found 84 per cent with soil losses greater than 12 tonnes per hectare.[4]

In tropical regions, erosion is aggravated by the pressure of increasing population, rising demand for agricultural products, the inequitable distribution of land (which forces the poor on to land unsuitable for cultivation) and poor farming techniques. According to FAO figures, there are currently 1.5 billion hectares (3.7 billion acres) of arable land under cultivation. Soil erosion removes the productivity of an estimated 5 to 7 million hectares (12 to 17 million acres) of that land annually. Even if existing cultivated land is farmed more intensively, plans to bring an additional 200 million hectares (495 million acres) into production by the year 2000 would, says FAO, only just compensate for the amount of soil lost in that time if degradation goes unchecked.

There are additional indirect costs, the most serious of which is the siltation of dams and reservoirs by the soil washed into rivers. About 139 million tonnes of silt enter the Aswan High Dam in Egypt every year, at which rate the dam will be completely filled with silt within a century. Siltation also clogs up essential irrigation systems, undermining attempts to increase food production, and reduces the navigability of major waterways such as the Panama Canal. Unless siltation of the Panama Canal is controlled, more and more shipping will have to make a detour around Cape Horn, or the canal will have to be dredged at considerable expense.

Desertification

Desert conditions are spreading. A decade ago, the word 'desertification' was barely heard. Then came the 1968-73 Sahelian drought. Droughts are not uncommon in the area (along the southern border of the Sahara), but increasing human pressure had magnified a 'natural' problem into a human problem of tragic proportions. Human pressure, specifically over-cultivation, over-grazing, clearance of tree and plant cover, and careless irrigation, all of which remove protective vegetative cover from the land, have brought desertification to more than 100 countries. Land is so degraded by human activity that it loses its fertility and its economic value.[5] Desertification occurs not only along the margins of existing deserts, but can also spring up even in areas with plenty of rain.

Despite the tragedy of the Sahel drought, desertification continues apace. Every year, another 6.2 million hectares (15.4 million acres) – an area twice the size of Belgium – is affected. The UN Conference on Desertification, held in 1977, discussed many of the causes and drew up a plan of action aimed at controlling the process by the turn of the century. But by 1984 the UN Environment Programme had concluded that too little was being done and that the target was unrealistic.[6] One reason was that the South was giving too little attention to the problem. Not only is desertification a long-term problem that has to compete for scarce resources and finances with all the short-term problems that face Third World countries, but it also mainly affects rural people who have little political power. For the North, desertification is a distant problem, and many would rather give aid to developing countries to finance prestige projects such as roads and factories than give money to help curb the spread of desert conditions. An area of two billion hectares (five billion acres) – twice the size of Canada – could ultimately be turned into desert unless the process is halted.

Forests

Forests not only provide timber for a wide variety of essential products, ranging from fuel to paper, but they also support animal and plant life, soak up rainwater (preventing floods), absorb carbon dioxide, and bind soil (preventing erosion). Yet they are being burned and cut down to make way for farmland, roads, and towns. In 1955, forests covered more than one-quarter of the earth's land surface. By 1977 they covered only one-fifth.[7] Some countries have fared better than others. While countries such as China and South Korea have increased their forest cover in recent years, the forests of Asia, Africa and Latin America are shrinking by more than seven million hectares (17 million acres) annually.[8]

While most of Europe still has more than 20 per cent forest cover, Britain has just 9 per cent (although that is almost double the figure in 1895). The death of 11 million English elms in the 1970s came as a shock to many, but British farmers have probably removed twice as many deciduous trees without public comment. Devon lost one-fifth of its woodland between 1952 and 1972.[9] Nearly one-third of our remaining ancient woods have either been cleared or have been replanted with conifers since the war. Anyone taking heart from figures that show an increase in British woodland cover should remember that much of this is due to the extension of commercial conifer plantations, using non-native species of tree. It is a sobering thought to remember that the majestic 'wilderness' of much of the Scottish highlands is in fact denuded wasteland stripped of its natural forest cover.

Nowhere is the problem of deforestation more marked than in tropical moist forests, the greatest of all concentrations of animal and plant life. While one hectare (2.5 acres) of English woodland may contain ten different tree species, a hectare of rain forest may contain as many as 200. The rain forests of South East Asia are thought to contain more than 25,000 flowering plant species, half of which are unique to the region.

Tropical forests provide not only timber but crops such as rubber, cocoa, coffee, many nuts and fruits, and essential drugs. Because rain forests have taken millions of years to develop, once removed, they are effectively gone for ever. But this has not discouraged developers from clearing them at an annual rate of 11 million hectares (27.5 million acres) for agriculture, grazing, settlement and logging. A 1975 UN study showed that remaining tropical moist forests covered 378 million hectares (935 million acres) – or only 60 per cent of their natural area.

The figures for tropical moist forest removal were given a huge boost in 1983-84 by one of the world's biggest-ever forest fires, which destroyed an area of rain forest bigger than Taiwan and became so hot that, in places, the earth itself ignited. The fire, in the Indonesian state of Kalimantan on the island of Borneo, is thought to have been started by a combination of drought, fires started by cultivators clearing land for crops, and the waste timber left behind by selective logging in the area. Apart from the immediate destruction to wildlife and habitat, the fire could have a long-term effect on local weather patterns.[10]

Urban development

Urban development is spreading, with up to 300,000 hectares (740,000 acres) of prime agricultural land alone being buried under roads, factories and houses in the North alone, every year. That is equivalent to an area nearly the size of Belgium being urbanized in the past decade. The catchment areas of cities are expanding as more people move to commuter-belt towns and villages, demanding new roads and transport services, ancillary services, and recreational facilities. Meanwhile, city centres are dying and the proportion of derelict land within the cities is growing. In the South, the urban population is exploding. In 1950, Buenos Aires was the only Third World city with more than four million people; today there are 22 (compared with 16 in the North); by the year 2000 there are expected to be more than 60. London, in 1950 the second most populous city in the world, will, it is estimated, have fallen to 28th place in the world rankings, having been overtaken by cities such as Mexico City, Sao Paulo, Bombay, Jakarta and Cairo.[11]

Urban spread in the North uses up agricultural lands, forests and natural habitats, creates demand for more services (food, water, energy, and raw materials), produces increasing volumes of sewage and garbage that have to be disposed of, and generates pollution of all kinds that has to be

51

controlled. In the South, the lack of adequate housing encourages the spread of mean shanty towns largely unprovided with basic services. Good agricultural land also disappears; Global 2000 reported that the area of irrigated land in Egypt has barely changed in 20 years because old irrigated land is lost to development as fast as new land is irrigated. One estimate[12] is that, unless present trends change, development in the last quarter of the century will swallow up 25 million hectares (62 million acres) of cropland – 2 per cent of the world total – which is enough to feed 84 million people.

Inland waters

Inland waters are being polluted. Less than one-hundredth of 1 per cent of the earth's water is fresh. A small fraction of that is safe enough to drink or wash with. Less than half the people living in the South have access to fresh water supplies, and only one in four has adequate sanitary facilities; for them, fresh water is always scarce. In contrast, most countries in the North have fresh water on tap, but, as the droughts of 1976 and 1984 showed, even Britain's supplies are not unlimited.

Reservoirs and treatment plants have to be built to produce fresh, clean water; waste water containing sewage, chemicals and detergents is often pumped untreated into rivers and the sea. While the Thames and other rivers have been cleaned up, and more controls have been placed on discharge from industry, 20 per cent of Britain's sewage is still not treated. (Some countries have an even worse record: 90 per cent of Belgium's sewage is untreated.) New sources of relatively uncontrolled pollution have been identified. The run-off of fertilizers and pesticides from farmland, and of chemicals and poisons from city streets, still pollutes European rivers. Acid rain and siltation from soil erosion pose additional threats. In the South the position is worsened because there are fewer controls on industry and often serious contamination from sewage.

Wilderness

Wilderness is disappearing. There is still true wilderness (land effectively untouched by human activity) in the Americas, Africa, Asia and Australasia, but very little in Europe and effectively none at all in Britain. Traces of pollution have been found even in the Arctic and Antarctic. In the North, almost every hectare has been turned over to some form of use, whether a city or nature reserve. In the South, the demand for fuelwood and for land to feed growing populations has led to inroads being made on remaining natural habitat. For all the benefits of nature reserves, national parks and other protected areas, many now amount to little more than open air zoos – the last pockets and parcels of land left for wildlife and nature.

THE OCEANS

Despite research and exploration, very little is known about the oceans outside coastal waters and fishing grounds. The oceans cover seven-tenths of the planet, exert enormous influence on climate, are home to abundant animal and plant species, contain valuable minerals and chemicals, are a vital means of transport, and could be a source of wave-generated energy. But they remain alien, and continue to be used as a dumping ground for everything from sewage to radioactive nuclear waste, and as a seemingly endless source of fish. Because all but coastal zones are outside national jurisdiction, there is little control over how the seas are used.

Over-fishing

Over-fishing has been a problem for centuries. One of the earliest recorded declines of a major fishery was that off the coast of Newfoundland in the seventeenth century. The effects of over-fishing have been particularly graphically demonstrated during the past two decades. Fish and seafood account for about 6 per cent of the protein in human diet as a whole (compared with 16 per cent in meat and 9.5 per cent in dairy products), but traditional fishing nations derive up to one-third of their animal protein from fish. In the period 1948-68, the world fish catch climbed at a steady 6 to 7 per cent per annum. It fell off during the 1970s, then grew to its present annual average of 75 million tonnes. The growth rate is now about 1 to 2 per cent per annum, but, worldwide, the supply of fish per head of human population has decreased. The slowing in the growth rate has been partly a result of the scarcity of unexploited and readily accessible species, but mainly because of over-fishing.

Like all renewable resources, fisheries need to be managed carefully to give them time to restock and maintain their numbers. If too many fish are caught, there will be too few left to breed and replace the stocks. The most common practice to date has been to fish an area until its stocks are gone and then move on. FAO undertakes annual assessments of the status of the world's fisheries; although it calculates that the world's fisheries could probably survive an annual catch of 90 to 100 million tonnes, over-fishing has already resulted in at least 25 of the world's major fishing grounds becoming seriously depleted, including Britain's major fishing grounds in the north-east Atlantic. The world's fish catch in 1979 was only 75 to 80 per cent of what it might have been with more careful management.[13] The worst affected fisheries are those in seas dominated by industrialized countries: the north Atlantic, the north Pacific, and the Mediterranean. Even catches of staple North Atlantic fish such as cod, haddock and halibut are on the decline; because too many cod were caught in the 1960s, cod catches in the north-west Atlantic are only one-third of their estimated potential, and cod is more expensive as a result. Over-fishing of herring led to a ban on herring catches by British fishermen between 1977 and 1984.

The most dramatic example of the effects of over-fishing was the collapse in the 1970s of the world's biggest fishery: the Peruvian anchovy catch.[14] In the 1960s it accounted for as much as one-fifth of the world's fish catch, encouraged by the demand for fishmeal from European, American and Japanese customers. Despite warnings, the annual catch repeatedly exceeded the maximum sustainable yield (safe limit) of 9.5 million tonnes. This, combined with a shift in ocean currents, caused a collapse in 1972. As late as 1979 the annual catch was still only 1.4 million tonnes, and sardines had moved in to fill the ecological vacuum left behind.

Another marine environmental problem is the well-documented plight of marine mammals (whales, dolphins, seals and porpoises), singled out for public support because of their intelligence, gentleness and – it cannot be denied – public relations value to conservation groups. Despite growing concern, many whales are still not protected and are in danger of being hunted to the point of extinction. Some – such as the bowhead and the humpback – are so low in numbers that even if all hunting was banned their numbers would keep falling off for several years. Hunting is not the only threat. Humpbacks, for example, are having to compete with fishermen for capelin, a small fish that is their main food source. A moratorium on whaling was finally achieved in 1982, but the decisions of the International Whaling Commission are not binding on their members, and enforcing the ban may be difficult.

Accidental killing also takes its toll on marine life. For every tonne of shrimp caught, for example, at least three tonnes of dead fish are dumped back into the sea. That means that at least 6.5 million tonnes of dead fish are thrown away every year as a result of shrimp trawling alone. Marine mammals and seabirds also suffer – whales, dolphins, turtles, sea cows and seals are frequently accidentally caught and die. At least a million seabirds are accidentally killed every year.

The reduced growth of conventional fisheries led to an upsurge of interest during the early 1970s in Antarctic krill, a small shrimp-like animal found in the Southern Ocean. In the 1970s there were estimates that catches of 110 to 150 million tonnes were sustainable.[15] But krill form the main link in the Southern Ocean food chain, and any major krill fishing could threaten the entire Antarctic ecosystem, particularly the blue, fin, humpback, minke and sei whales which feed on krill.

Marine pollution
Marine pollution has not turned out to be as serious as was once predicted.[16] Oil pollution has increased, it is true, but seemingly as yet without causing lasting damage. The effects of oil spills have been dramatic and visible enough to compel governments to take action, and there are now various international laws and conventions dealing with marine pollution, and with the dumping of toxic waste at sea. The United Nations Environment Programme's Regional Seas Programme is helping to clean up the Mediterranean, and providing a model for other regional seas such as the Red Sea and the Caribbean.

While the open ocean is relatively untouched, it is a very different story with coastal waters. Because most marine life is concentrated along coastlines, and coastal ecosystems support most major fisheries, there is cause for serious concern. Most pollution reaches the sea via rivers, drainage and the dumping of waste. Sewage, toxic chemicals, petrochemical waste and other effluent is being dumped into the sea by industries and local municipalities, killing marine life and often accumulating in fish, making them unfit to eat. The Minamata tragedy showed how seafood can become contaminated. Shellfish are particularly prone to accumulating heavy metals and other toxic wastes. More than one-quarter of the shellfish grounds off 13 US states were closed to commercial harvesting in the late 1970s because of contamination.[17] Shellfish found off Mexico, Tokyo Bay in Japan, Jakarta Bay in Indonesia, and Hong Kong have been found to contain dangerous amounts of polychlorinated biphenyls (PCBs, which are toxic and long-lasting industrial chemicals) and heavy metals such as cadmium, chromium and mercury. Despite the lessons of Minamata, mercury levels in many Japanese coastal waters remain dangerously high.

Development

Development is destroying marine life. Dredging for landfill, anchorages and channels, and the relatively recent increase in the exploitation of minerals, oil and gas from the sea, all take their toll. Coastal wetlands (made up of estuaries, salt marshes and mangrove swamps) are particularly vulnerable. Up to 80 per cent of commercial marine fisheries depend on estuarine ecosystems for much of their life cycle, yet coastal wetlands are often chosen as prime sites for the siting of industry and for the 'reclamation' of land for other uses. They are drained for agriculture, polluted by waste disposal, and disrupted by water supply schemes, recreation and tourism. The annual area of land reclaimed by field drainage in England and Wales alone is as much as 100,000 hectares (250,000 acres).[18]

Tropical coral reefs have been compared to tropical moist forests in their complexity and diversity. They provide self-regenerating breakwaters that create secure nurseries for marine life, supporting up to 3,000 different species. But development, particularly in relation to tourism, is causing their destruction. Corals and shells are stripped to be sold to tourists, or to be used in cement and building materials. Sewage and other pollution are killing off reef life. Lagoons are deepened and widened for marinas and harbours. Inland soil erosion causes silt to be washed down to the sea by rivers. Reefs contain abundant animal and plant life, and not only support coastal fisheries but often form islands in themselves – more than 400 islands throughout the tropics would not exist without reef-building corals.[19]

THE ATMOSPHERE

Air pollution began with the smoking wood fires of primitive societies, but only became a problem with the advent of the industrial revolution. In terms of its immediacy and visibility, few environmental issues have had more impact. The foul air of industrial Britain in the nineteenth century inspired social reform, the literature of Dickens, and emigration. Smog – smoke from coal-burning houses and factories which combined with fog – produced an atmosphere so foul that as late as the early 1950s thousands of Londoners were dying from its effects.

The major sources of atmospheric pollution are the gases and particles given off by the burning of fossil fuels, smoke from forest and grassland fires, and ploughing and over-grazing that releases dust into the atmosphere. Because its effects have been so immediate, and have therefore generated public concern, much has been done to tackle air pollution. Clean air laws have cleared the skies over many European and American cities. Levels of sulphur dioxide in the air, caused by coal-burning, have declined, and emission of smoke has been curbed: London now has 70 per cent more hours of sunshine in December than it did in 1958, largely owing to the fact that Londoners no longer burn coal in such large quantities. The 1963 Nuclear Test Ban Treaty helped to curb radioactive contamination of the atmosphere. According to the US Environmental Protection Agency, the levels of strontium-90 and caesium-137 in the atmosphere, after peaking in 1964, fell by 84 per cent and 94 per cent respectively by 1978. Lead-free petrol is already widely available in the United States, and Europe is due to follow suit in 1987.

However, there have been some new problems. Taller smokestacks have been introduced to disperse the sulphur dioxide given off by industry in England and Wales to the winds, but those winds have been carrying the sulphur dioxide north to Scotland and Scandinavia. There, it reacts with water in the air to cause acid rain – rain that is often more acid than vinegar – which kills and deforms fish in Swedish and Norwegian lakes and rivers, trees, and corrodes metal and stone. Third World countries undergoing their own industrial revolutions now suffer many of the problems partly or wholly eliminated in the North. Acid rain is becoming a problem in the industrial centres of countries such as Brazil, Zambia and South Africa. In many Third World cities, heart and lung diseases linked to air pollution are on the rise. The dependence on firewood as a major source of energy is causing heavy smogs over cities, especially those with large slums.

City smogs remain a problem in both North and South. Unlike London, Los Angeles has not made much progress in controlling air pollution. Despite its notoriety, little is known about its causes, thought to lie in a combination of the physical location of the city and the dependence of its residents on cars. The city's smog problems were given more publicity in August 1984 with fears for the effects it might have on the performances of athletes at the Los Angeles Olympics. The month before, a heat wave caused levels of smog in Athens to rise so alarmingly that the government had to impose emergency measures to protect the health of Athenians and maintain its own political credibility. Half the private cars on the streets were ordered off for 48 hours and industries were told to cut fuel consumption by 30 per cent. About 500 people were hospitalized with respiratory complaints in the space of two days.[20]

Another problem is the possible threat posed by aerosols to the stratospheric ozone, an unstable form of oxygen which absorbs ultraviolet solar radiation. Many aerosol cans, refrigerants and solvents contain chlorofluorocarbons (CFCs) which, in sufficient quantities, can destroy ozone. Any increase in the amount of ultraviolet radiation reaching the surface of the earth could harm animal and plant life. Among other things, there is some evidence that ultraviolet radiation is linked to skin cancer.

One of the major drawbacks in assessing the impact of pollution problems on the atmosphere is the lack of data. Surface weather records have been kept for more than 200 years, but many of the earliest weather stations were built in or near towns so their records were influenced by the effects of urban development. Similarly, there are very few stations based over the oceans. Atmospheric conditions vary enormously in time and place, making it difficult to predict changes. Research efforts have been redoubled in the past two decades with projects such as the Global Atmospheric Research Programme, run by the World Meteorological Programme and the International Council of Scientific Unions.

ENERGY

Encouraged by the ready availability of cheap fuel, energy consumption grew steadily after the war, particularly in the North. Total commercial energy consumption in 1950 was 2,500 million tonnes of coal equivalent (tce) – by 1970 it had risen to 6,500 million tce. At the same time there was a marked swing away from coal – which in 1920 provided 80 per cent of world energy consumption but by 1970 was down to 35 per cent – to oil. Consumption of liquid fuels, gas and electricity all trebled between 1960 and 1978.

All the more reason why the energy crisis of the 1970s and rising oil prices had such an impact, and why they put such economic pressure on most countries, particularly those in the South. People began to become convinced of the need both to conserve existing sources of energy and look for new ones. How have we responded? By using even more energy. World commercial energy consumption rose by 34 per cent between 1970 and 1979 (although this was an improvement on the previous decade, when it rose by nearly 60 per cent) and electricity production increased by 60 per cent. About 80 per cent of the increase was in the North.

An encouraging development has been the reduction of oil consumption by most industrialized countries. No country has a better record than Britain, which has cut oil consumption by more than a quarter since 1973. But the North, with 30 per cent of the world's population, still consumes 80 per cent of the world's commercial energy, mainly because there are so many private cars on the road, so many energy-intensive industries, and such ready and convenient access to as much electricity and natural gas as is needed in the home. The average European uses 15 times as much energy as the average African or Asian, and is doing little to change his or her habits. Despite crises and shortages, wastefulness is a growing problem. The fact that the South only accounts for 20 per cent of the world's commercial energy consumption disguises its growing demand for non-commercial fuels such as wood, charcoal, crop wastes and dung, which account for between 30 per cent and 95 per cent of total energy used in the Third World. Demand for fuelwood is increasing, leading in turn to widespread clearance of forests and scrubland, and worsening levels of smoke pollution.

Trying to forecast how long oil, gas and coal resources will last is a difficult and uncertain exercise. For example, *The Ecologist*'s report 'A Blueprint for Survival' warned in 1972 that, if consumption rates continued to grow exponentially as they had since 1960, the world's natural gas would be exhausted by 1986 and the world's petroleum by 1992. Forecasts of how long coal reserves will last vary from 800 years to 4,000 years. The only general certainty is that shortages of fossil fuels will not begin to make themselves felt globally until well into the next century.

But this is no cause for complacency. Consider the short- and medium-term problems of continuing to use fossil fuels.

In the first place, pollution will continue to be a hazard. Exhaust fumes create air pollution and introduce toxic substances such as lead, hydrocarbons and carbon monoxide into the air. Sulphur dioxide emitted by coal-burning power stations is creating acid rain that kills life in lakes and forests and corrodes railway tracks and stone buildings. The transport of oil by sea creates the ever-present danger of oil pollution.

Second, the distribution of fossil fuels is unequal. Britain is an oil producer, but many countries are not and find the economic burden of importing oil far too much to bear. Many countries in the South now spend between one-quarter and two-thirds of their foreign currency earnings on oil imports. Britain's oil supply will eventually run out and its population will then start to feel the economic pressures of buying oil. Britain's natural gas is projected to run out by the mid-1990s and it will have to import more or start to extract it from coal.

Given that all fossil fuels will eventually run out, it is inevitable that we must sooner or later start using alternative fuels. There have been experiments with solar energy, energy from the wind and waves, from decaying plant matter, and from other sources but it is unlikely that any of these sources of energy (except perhaps solar power) will be used commercially on any significant scale this century, despite the fact that they are cheaper and more versatile than existing sources of commercial energy. Two countries which are exceptions to the rule are Brazil and Zimbabwe which lead the world in the use of ethanol (ethyl alcohol) mixed with petrol. Conventional car engines can run on a mix of 20 per cent ethanol/80 per cent petrol, without any adjustments needed and in Zimbabwe all commercial petrol has this mix. Brazil launched its fuel alcohol programme in 1975 when oil imports began to place a heavy burden on the economy. By 1985 it hopes to produce enough ethanol to meet half its fuel needs.

One of the only alternatives to coal-powered electricity generating stations to be used commercially is nuclear power (hydro-electricity provides only 6 per cent of the world's total primary energy, well below its potential). Nuclear power's environmental effects make it an unwelcome alternative. The anti-nuclear power movement has been heartened by the recent conclusion that nuclear power is less economically attractive than once anticipated. After reaching a peak in 1973, orders for new nuclear power reactors declined. By 1979 they provided about 8 per cent of the world's electricity (14 per cent in Britain), a percentage, however, that is projected to increase. The nuclear power debate of the 1960s, which centred on the safety of nuclear installations, the risks to human life of exposure to low levels of radiation, and the environmental problems of dealing with radioactive waste, broadened during the 1970s to include discussion on the use of nuclear material for non-peaceful purposes and the security risks associated with nuclear plants. Opposition to nuclear power has been fuelled by incidents such as Three Mile Island in March 1979 and, more recently, by Greenpeace's attempt in 1984 to seal off the pipe discharging waste from the Sellafield power station into the Irish Sea, which is now one of the most radioactively polluted seas in the world.

The most fundamental alternative to fossil fuels and nuclear power is energy conservation. In Britain at the present time, more energy is wasted than is used effectively. Power stations are not always energy-effective, and more than half our primary energy is used to heat buildings, where much of the heat escapes through roofs, walls and windows. There is considerable scope for using existing sources of energy more economically, so much so that energy conservation in itself is increasingly described as a major alternative energy 'source'. Energy conservation saves more money than it costs to initiate, and is within reach of everyone who uses commercial energy (see Chapter 5).

WILDLIFE AND HABITATS

Despite the efforts of wildlife conservation groups, and their success in pulling some threatened species back from the brink of extinction, the problem of threatened wildlife is now far greater than ever before. This is partly because the diversity and degree of the threats posed are accelerating, and partly because much more is known about the kinds of threats wildlife faces. In the last two decades, there have been two major changes in the way the wildlife problem has been seen.

First, conservation has replaced preservation as the favoured solution to the problem. Second, until a decade ago, much of the attention concentrated on a relatively limited group of mammals and birds. Today, as ecologists learn more about the natural world, and conservationists are guided less by the public relations value of the more attractive mammals and birds in raising funds and more by the need to manage representative ecosystems, so the wider proportions of the overall problem are becoming clear. Plants, amphibians, reptiles, insects and other classes are finally being given the attention they deserve, and the need to see wildlife conservation in the context of the other demands made of land and resources is being acknowledged.

Until relatively recently, for example, national parks were seen as the definitive answer to wildlife conservation. They are now seen as increasingly untenable, especially in Third World countries with growing populations where demand for farmland is strong. Local people need a lot of convincing before they agree to put the welfare of animals before their own immediate survival. As Erik Eckholm observed: 'An animal cannot be saved apart from its habitat, and natural areas cannot last as fortress islands in seas of hungry people. Where large numbers lack a means to make a decent living, some are sure to invade national parks to grow food and cut wood'.[22] Poaching, for example, will never be curbed until national parks are supported by local people and trade in animal products is effectively controlled.

The wildlife issue is still largely speculative. Far less is known about wildlife than most people believe. About 1.5 million species of animals and plants have so far been identified, and of most of those little more is known than their location. Most current estimates put the total number of species at anything from three to ten million. Very little is known, for instance, of the number of species to be found in the tropical moist forests or oceans. IUCN currently estimates that about 1,000 bird and mammal species are threatened with extinction, and about 10 per cent (20 to 30,000) of the world's plant species.

Hard evidence in the form of population numbers, current threats and future prospects exist for only a fraction of the IUCN-listed species, making such figures misleading and largely meaningless. It is more than likely that there have been many extinctions that have gone unnoticed because the species involved have never been identified. Given the number of well-documented threatened species, such as the giant panda, the Arabian oryx and the California condor, IUCN estimates that one species or sub-species of higher animal becomes extinct every year. Other estimates put the rate at closer to one animal or plant species every day.[23]

The bulk of the world's wildlife is threatened in varying degrees by human activity: the spread of human settlement (farms, towns, cities), forest clearance, pollution, and trade in endangered species. Of the IUCN-listed threatened species, 67 per cent are threatened by habitat destruction, 37 per cent by over-exploitation, 19 per cent by the effects of introduced species, and 9 per cent by other causes.[24]

The past decade has seen considerable growth in the number of wildlife conservation groups, in the quality and quantity of ecological research, in the amount of money raised for conservation, in the number of international conventions and laws, in the number of protected areas, in publicity for conservation, and in the newly emerging sense of the importance of research into and conservation of lower animal forms, the plant kingdom, and habitats and ecosystems as a whole. But the most significant development has been the realization that wildlife cannot be preserved in isolation, and that no amount of money or legislation is going to protect individual species until the social, economic and political pressures that threaten habitat are resolved. Attitudes towards wildlife conservation are moving beyond emotional appeals on to hard-headed practical reasoning.

EFFECTING THE SOLUTIONS

Environmentalists constantly expose themselves to the charge of being dismal doommongers: of dealing only in bad news. Given the catalogue of damage, degradation and waste that characterizes the way we treat the environment, it is often hard to present any more positive picture. Some damage is irreparable: the passenger pigeon, for example, and the dodo have gone for ever, as have many hectares of tropical forest. It will take hundreds of years to replace lost top soil, and thousands of years to make radioactive waste safe.

But the fact is that the environment has become a public issue and more people now realize that there is a problem is progress. The amount of environmental legislation is growing. The interests and influence of environmental pressure groups are expanding. Most countries have state environmental departments and in some countries the environment has entered mainstream politics. In 1983, the West German Greens capitalized on the new environmental interest by winning seats in the Bundestag. Finland elected Greens to its parliament, and in Austria, although the Greens were unable to win seats, they won enough votes to prevent the government party from winning a majority. In 1984, West Germany, Belgium and the Netherlands returned Greens to the European Parliament. And the intricacies of European relations finally persuaded Margaret Thatcher in 1984 to hold briefing sessions on acid rain.

More is known about the causes of the problems, which makes it easier to take effective action. However, one characteristic of environmental deterioration is that it is a gradual process, and very often becomes visible only over a long-term period: forests do not disappear overnight; the population of African elephants will not be here today and gone tomorrow. The possibility of enough carbon dioxide entering the atmosphere to make the polar ice-caps melt is so distant and extreme that most people would relegate the idea to the ranks of science fiction. Few people would drive their cars less in order to stave off an event which might occur several centuries hence.

There are two preconditions to the solution of most environmental problems. First, there needs to be a long-term view and commitment. It is human instinct to cure rather than prevent, and to take the short-term view. Most people are moved to take action to prevent disasters only once one has actually happened. It took the Aberfan disaster to move people to make slag heaps safe. It took the Torrey Canyon to draw the British government's attention to the dangers of oil spills. It took London smogs to bring home to people the dangers of air pollution.

Second, solving environmental problems requires an understanding of the links between cause and effect. The environmental movement as a whole still concentrates its wrath on the direct perpetrators of environmental damage, whether oil companies, farmers, car manufacturers, or multinationals. Too rarely is the role of the individual consumer emphasized. Yet each consumer is at the peak of a pyramid of resource demand and consumption that is often the root cause of environmental degradation. For example:

· The average British car consumes nearly 1,360 litres (300 gallons) of petrol every year. Anyone who uses a car causes increases in the amounts of lead and sulphur and carbon dioxide in the air, encourages the oil spills that pollute estuaries and kill tens of thousands of seabirds annually, contributes to fluctuations in the price of oil, and creates the demand for more roads and parking lots.
· Anyone who uses electricity increases the amount of coal burned by coal-fired power stations, the amount of sulphur dioxide released into the atmosphere and the amount of acid rain that falls, thereby strengthening government arguments in favour of nuclear power.
· Anyone who throws out glass bottles instead of recycling them encourages the quarrying of sand, limestone and soda ash, and increases the amount of energy consumed by the glass industry. Anyone who throws out paper instead of recycling it contributes to the clearance of forests and their conversion from natural woodland to commercial plantations.

These are simplified examples. There are many other factors that have to be taken into account, including marketing strategies, the built-in obsolescence of products, the achievement of status and personal ambition, and government support for greater industrial and agricultural output. But the position of consumers at the peak of the pyramid of demand provides them with considerable influence over the way the earth's natural resources are used and the way the environment is affected. Once the links are understood, everyone is capable of lessening the negative impact of his or her way of life on the environment – and *without* any major changes in lifestyles. We have become used to over-consuming and wasting resources. We need to become used to using resources economically and efficiently.

Until we start questioning our way of life and amending our demands, both as individuals and communities, environmental deterioration will continue, shortages will worsen, and prices of resources will rise. As individual consumers we create a demand that suppliers endeavour to meet at almost any cost. Each one of us is responsible for this. We are all part of the problem until we become part of the solution.

REFERENCES

1 Eckholm, Erik (1982) *Down to Earth*. Pluto Press, London
2 Earthscan (1984) *Cropland or wasteland: The problems and promises of irrigation*. Earthscan Press Briefing Document No 38, London
3 Parrington, J R *et al* (1983) Asian Dust: Seasonal transport to the Hawaiian islands. In *Science*, 8 April
4 *The Global 2000 Report to the President* (1982). Penguin, Harmondsworth
5 Grainger, Alan (1982) *Desertification*. Earthscan, London
6 Tolba, M K (1984) *Desertification is stoppable*. Speech delivered to UNEP Governing Council, Nairobi
7 Global 2000 *op cit*
8 Caufield, Catherine (1982) *Tropical Moist Forests*. Earthscan, London
9 Rose, Chris (1984) Wildlife: The battle for the British countryside. In Wilson, Des (ed) *The Environmental Crisis*. Heinemann, London
10 Johnson, Brian (1984) *Fire without Smoke?* Earthscan, London
11 Earthscan (1983) *Urban land and shelter for the poor*. Earthscan Press Briefing Document No 35, London
12 Brown, Lester (1978) *The Worldwide Loss of Cropland*. Worldwatch Paper No 24, Washington DC

13 FAO (1979) *Review of the state of world fishery resources.* Committee on Fisheries: Thirteenth Session. Rome

14 Gulland, John (1975) The harvest of the sea. In Murdoch, W W (ed) *Resources, Pollution and Society.* Sunderland, Massachusetts

15 Mitchell, Barbara and Tinker, Jon (1980) *Antarctica and its Resources.* Earthscan, London

16 Eckholm, Erik *op cit*

17 Ibid

18 Baldock, David (1984) *Wetland Drainage in Europe.* IIED/IEEP, London

19 Salvat, Bernard (1979) Trouble in paradise, part two: Coral reef parks and reserves. In *Parks* 4:1-4

20 *The Times* (1984) 18 July

21 Global 2000 *op cit*

22 Eckholm *op cit*

23 Myers, Norman (1979) *The Sinking Ark.* Pergamon, Oxford

24 Allen, Robert (1980) *How to Save the World.* Kogan Page, London

THE INTERNATIONAL ENVIRONMENT

3

Most environmental problems – and their solutions – are local or national. Disappearing British hedgerows are a British problem. The dumping of toxic wastes in the United States is an American problem (unless the United States dumps its wastes in international waters). Only Japanese law can control the pollution of Japanese coastal waters.

But many of the most critical environmental problems go beyond national frontiers. Some, such as soil erosion, deforestation, and over-fishing are universal. More significantly, many problems have their causes in one country and their effects in others. In the case of pollution, prevailing winds can blow contaminants across continents, and sea currents can wash contamination from one shore to another. With many other international environmental problems, the links lie in trade. On a planet where the distribution of natural resources is unequal, trade is essential. Demand for a resource in one country is met by its development and exploitation in another. But over-consumption and waste in one country can also be translated into environmental degradation in another, not only through consumption but also as a consequence of consumption.

Britain is particularly poorly endowed in natural resources: it has oil, coal and fertile farmland, but has to rely heavily on the import of most other raw materials. The value of colonies as sources of raw materials was one of the main reasons for the development of the British empire. Four hundred years ago, Britain and its Northern temperate neighbours began using their military and technological power to control world trade, and have retained much of this control to the present day. Nowhere are the environmental implications of international trade more forcefully illustrated than in the relationship between North and South.

THE NORTH-SOUTH IMBALANCE

The North has long taken the South for granted. Until the end of the colonial era in the 1950s and 1960s, the prevailing attitude of colonial powers towards their colonies was that they were there to be exploited. This view lay behind the sixteenth and seventeenth century extraction of South American gold and silver, the seventeenth and eighteenth century East Indies spice trade, the nineteenth century Chinese opium trade, and – the most naked form of exploitation – the slave trade. More recently, prime agricultural land in the colonies was made available for settlers to buy and develop, and the mineral and agricultural resources were exported back to the North in their raw form to feed the North's manufacturing industries. The flow was largely one-way, with little exchange. Local people were regarded as a cheap source of labour, had access to few of their country's resources or the benefits they provided, and had little opportunity to be educated, learn a profession, or achieve senior administrative posts.

Following independence, the priority for most emerging countries was to redress the balance by taking control of their resources and thereby reaping the benefits, educating their people, ensuring a more equitable distribution of land, and negotiating fair trading terms with the North. Their aim was to achieve economic, political and social parity with the North. The results have been variable.

Land

Land has not always been fairly redistributed, and rapid population growth has led to increased demand for resources. The poorest people in the world are those who live in the rural areas of the South. Few own the land they till, and most are subsistence farmers living from hand to mouth. The land is often owned by a wealthy elite. FAO estimates, for example, that 93 per cent of the arable land in Latin America is owned by only 7 per cent of the landowners. In Kenya, half the farmers till just 15 per cent of the cultivable land. Lack of land and training compels the poorest farmers to make do with what little is available. This may make them clear a tract of forest, plough a steep mountain slope (leaving it open for rain to wash away the soil), over-graze semi-arid land and court the danger of desertification, or spill over into a national park or wildlife reserve.

Population growth

Population growth has made it almost impossible for governments in the South to keep up with the demands of their people. With some exceptions, population control is most successful where the economic benefits of development reach the most people. With the insecurity of an unstable economy, high infant mortality and poor life expectancy, most rural poor make sure they have large families so that enough children survive to become wage-earners or work the family plot.

Resources

Many resources have been nationalized, but Northern multinationals often retain a major – if not a controlling – interest. For example, 70 per cent of the world banana trade is controlled by three US multinationals: United Brands, Del Monte and Castle Cook. British-based companies such as Lyons, Liptons, Twinings and Brooke Bond dominate the international tea trade. Multinationals control between one-quarter and one-third of *all* world production. In 1976, the sales of their foreign affiliates were equal to the gross national product of all Third World countries except the oil exporters. Foreign industries are attracted to developing countries because of the lax environmental regulations which may allow them to build factories without the cost of installing anti-pollution measures or meeting environmental health standards.

Many industries – both foreign and national – still exploit cheap labour. The tea trade is an example of this. Britain is by far the world's largest importer of tea; the biggest exporters are Sri Lanka, India and Kenya. Despite a 50 per cent rise in productivity among tea pickers in Assam between 1961 and 1976, their basic wage rate actually fell by 10 per cent in real terms. British companies control about half the tea production in Assam. In 1979, tea pickers in India earned £13 per month; in Kenya they earned about £12 and in Sri Lanka about £7.[1]

Trade

Trade between North and South retains many of the imbalances of the colonial era. The trade in commodities is a prime example. Most of the South's export earnings (up to 80-90 per cent in some countries) come from commodities such as coffee, sugar, tea, cocoa, natural rubber, jute, nickel, copper and tin. The bulk of these are exported in their raw form, and most of the really profitable part of commodity trading – processing – takes place in the North, and it is the North which reaps the profits. For example, more than half of the world's bauxite (the ore from which aluminium is made) comes from the South, but the North has 90 per cent of the refining capacity. Raw bauxite earns Third World producers only 2 to 3 per cent of the price they would receive for processed aluminium. Manufacturing industries often account for less than 10 per cent of the gross domestic product of Third World countries, compared with 19 per cent in the UK, 22 per cent in the US, 30 per cent in Japan and 35 per cent in West Germany. The North frequently imposes tariffs to discourage the export of processed commodities and protect its own manufacturing industries. Hence the EEC imports rice duty free, but puts a 13 per cent tariff on processed rice and rice products. Untreated wood enters Australia duty free, but sawn timber faces a tariff of 7 to 14 per cent.[2]

Aid

Aid, insist the donor countries, is given to the South for humanitarian or moral reasons. But it is often given on condition that it is used to buy products from the donor country. It is rarely given to countries whose political views are very different from those of the donor country. Many donors give money to support their national interests in the recipient country. Much aid goes into relatively non-urgent prestige projects (such as new airports, super highways, new capital cities) and little into easing the plight of the people who really need help: the rural poor, who usually lack the political power to influence how the money is spent. Local people are rarely consulted about their needs, and are even more rarely involved in the planning, development or running of projects. To make matters worse, the South is becoming increasingly indebted to the North, often in staggering proportions: in 1984, Brazil owed the North $60 billion, and Mexico owed $90 billion.

Some of the responsibility for the failure of development plans rests with the Third World itself. Political instability, corruption, inefficiency and bureaucratic incompetence are all real problems – many of them are common to the North. But the South often finds its hands tied by the North, which not only consumes far more than its fair share of resources, but also capitalizes on the economic and political advantages it holds over the South, and puts obstacles in the Third World's path of progress. The North's deficit of natural resources is offset by its economic and political strength. The North has only 16 per cent of the world's population but has four-fifths of its income, 90 per cent of its manufacturing industries, and consumes 75 per cent of its food and 55 per cent of its commercial energy. In the North, the average person lives to about 70, and (in most countries) need never go hungry or lack shelter, medical care and education. The South, by contrast, is economically weak but rich in natural resources. Life expectancy is just over 50; one out of four children dies before the age of five in the poorest countries; one in five people suffers from undernutrition; and only one in two has the opportunity to become literate.[3]

This social and economic imbalance between North and South is, in turn, a fundamental cause of much of the environmental degradation that afflicts Third World countries. There are two main problems. First, as part of their programme of development, Third World countries have given priority to the rapid development and exploitation of their natural resources. Second, a combination of poverty and growing population has put increasing pressure on those natural resources.

[handwritten margin note: 2 Main 3rd World problems.]

There is one fundamental difference between environmental problems in the North and in the South. In the North, these problems arise mostly from decisions taken within the planning system of the country. With some exceptions, the North's environmental problems are self-inflicted and can theoretically be self-cured. In the South, by contrast, the environment is degraded as a result of circumstances that are often beyond the control of the country affected. The country may be poor, indebted to the North, and compelled to grow many of its crops for export. Because its people are poor and life expectancy is low, the birth rate is high. The population grows and puts more pressure on the land. In the struggle to survive, the welfare of the environment can seem a very distant concern. As Erik Eckholm observes: 'caught in endless cycles of hunger, illiteracy, exploitation, and disease, the absolute poor have no time to worry about global environmental trends ... Most of the rural poor live directly off the soils, forests, waters, and wildlife whose deterioration has become the object of so much international concern. Many are forced by circumstances beyond their control to destroy the very resources from which they must scrape their living'.[4]

· Land is eroded, degraded and turned into desert. Desertification and the effects of the Sahelian drought, for example, are made worse by the demand for land that compels nomadic farmers to over-graze and over-cultivate land. In their rush to start irrigation schemes, developers often forego the extra cost of installing adequate drains or training farmers to use the system. The result is that the soil often becomes waterlogged or salinized, the system is not maintained, irrigation water is unequally distributed, and disease breeds in stagnant irrigation ditches.

71

· Health is threatened by the lack of controls that attracts pollutive industries. A country may deliberately set low standards in order to attract investment. Pesticides banned in the North are often exported to the South. The World Health Organization (WHO) reports that up to 40 per cent of workers in some countries are poisoned by pesticides during the annual spraying season. Many Northern countries may ban or restrict dangerous pesticides, drugs and hazardous wastes, but will often allow their export. In April 1977, the United States banned the domestic sale of fire-resistant sleepwear after hearing evidence that the substance that gave it fire resistance, called TRI5, could be linked with cancer. Over the next nine months an estimated 2.4 million TRI5-treated baby pyjamas were exported to Latin America, Africa and Asia.[5]

The effect of different standards of industrial safety were tragically illustrated by the events at Bhopal, India, in December 1984. A cloud of poison gas – methyl isocyanate – escaped from a US chemical plant and drifted over nearby residential areas. More than 100,000 people inhaled the gas, of whom more than 2,000 died. More than half of those who died were children.

As smoking becomes less popular in the North, there is evidence that tobacco companies are expanding their markets in the South. The health risks of smoking are so well documented that the seven multinationals which control the tobacco trade scarcely bother to deny them, arguing instead that people should be free to smoke if they want to. Many of the cigarettes sold in the Third World appear to have higher tar and nicotine content than exactly the same brands sold in the North. One survey found that tar levels in four international brands were twice as high in the Philippines as in Britain.[6]

· Development projects rarely have the long-term benefits they were designed to have, mainly because they lack environmental safeguards. In 1983, the aid agencies of Denmark, Finland, Norway and Sweden published a report in which they argued that development aid projects that were not environmentally sustainable were a waste of money and had no long-term benefits. Sustainable development has become one of the catch phrases of the 1980s. It has been defined as the process of improving the living conditions of the poor majority while avoiding the destruction of natural resources, so that increases of production and improvements in living conditions can be sustained in the longer term.[7]

A World Bank study between 1971 and 1978 found that one in three of the World Bank projects reviewed had resulted in environmental problems of one kind or another. Of these, about one-quarter required special studies to identify the necessary safeguards. Among the problem projects were a Kenyan pulp and paper mill which discharged effluent into the Nzoia river, carrying it into Lake Victoria (thereby affecting Kenya, Uganda and Tanzania), and an irrigation system for a sugar plantation which could have aggravated the already serious incidence of the water-associated disease schistosomiasis (bilharzia).[8]

· Wildlife is threatened by the encroachments on its natural habitat of desperate farmers searching for land, of villagers in search of firewood to cook their food and heat their homes, of logging companies in search of new tracts of woodland, and of the flooding that can come in the wake of deforestation. For a destitute peasant farmer, the temptation to poach is often too hard to resist. To a starving family, wildlife conservation can seem like an expensive irrelevancy, of use only to rich tourists. Rhinos, tigers and other animals from Nepal's Chitwan National Park have caused widespread crop damage in local areas, and have killed people and livestock. Villagers resent being barred from the park's forests and grazing land, and many have been resettled. Tourism has brought few benefits and little local development. The revenue from tourism contributes less than one-quarter of the money spent by the Nepal government on the park.[9]

· Cities often seem to provide the opportunities unavailable to the poor in rural areas, and people flock there in search of jobs and security. But what they usually find is poverty, unemployment, disease, slums, too little land, few basic services, and little opportunity. In 1920, only 15 per cent of people in the South lived in urban settlements. By 1980, the proportion had risen to 41 per cent. The environment of the cities suffers as pollution and traffic increases. The health and safety of the people suffers as the environment deteriorates. Four-fifths of the population of Guayaquil, Ecuador's largest city, live in slums or shacks built on swamps or land subject to floods. Some of them live a 40-minute walk from dry land.

· Agriculture provides a major example of how trade inequalities contribute to environmental problems. A legacy of the colonial era was the specialization of many countries in a few cash crops (sugar from the Caribbean, cocoa from West Africa, and rubber from South East Asia).

Market forces have made it difficult for these countries to diversify and produce crops essential for home consumption. Their dependence on trade in cash crops committed them to make the export market their first priority. For most countries in the South, agriculture is the major activity. In Uganda it accounts for 82 per cent of the gross domestic product, and in Bangladesh, Ethiopia, Tanzania and Ghana it accounts for about half.[10] In Cuba, as much as 42 per cent of the land is given over to export crops.

problems

A number of problems arise out of specialization in one or two export crops. First, a single crop disease or natural disaster can decimate whole production centres. Second, the use of chemical-based pesticides and fertilizers is on the increase. Third, more than half the world's 77 food-exporting countries (including Ethiopia, Kenya, Chad and India) have too little food to feed their own people – yet they still export food. The poor are feeding the rich, and countries where undernutrition may already be rife are able to feed even fewer of their people.

The links between consumer demand in the North and environmental degradation in the South are complex, and the forces that dictate the imbalance are deep-rooted. Most British consumers regard environmental problems in, say, Costa Rica, Nepal or Indonesia as too remote and irrelevant to merit attention. Few actually see any link with themselves, and even fewer accept any responsibility. Yet there *are* links and we *are* responsible.

Consumer demand creates markets and trade which suppliers must satisfy, particularly if those suppliers depend on trade for most of their income. The South occasionally succeeds in making the North aware of the one-sidedness of the relationship between the two. The Third World countries that dominate the Organization of Petroleum Exporting Countries (OPEC) succeeded in 1973-74 with oil price rises that shook the North. But such instances are rare. The South remains overwhelmingly locked into an imbalanced relationship with the North which promises to bring it continuing social, economic, political and environmental upheaval. Consumers of the North helped to create the system and so are best placed to help amend it. In 1972, Barbara Ward coined the phrase 'Only One Earth' to emphasize how the choices available to us were limited by the carrying capacity of the planet we inhabit. In 1981, just before she died, she observed 'No matter how much we try to think of ourselves as separate sovereign entities, nature itself reminds us of 'man's basic unity'. [11]

This unity is illustrated not only in the consequences of the North-South imbalance, but also in transnational environmental problems between countries in North and South alike. Examples are rife: the way we use forests and energy, global threats to wildlife, the export of pollution, and the effects of one of the most direct forms of exploitation – tourism.

FORESTS

Estimates of the amount of forest in the world vary, but the figure now most widely accepted is 4.9 billion hectares (12 billion acres). The effects of growing population and rising demand are combining to reduce this total annually by an estimated 11.3 million hectares (27.9 million acres) – an area about the size of East Germany – in tropical areas alone. In 1960, forests covered one-quarter of the earth's land surface; today they cover one-fifth. [12]

Forests have several functions. As ecosystems they bind soil which might otherwise be eroded. Forests also control floods by soaking up rain and releasing it in springs, streams and groundwater. They recycle oxygen and nitrogen, absorb carbon dioxide and provide a habitat for animal and plant life. Many of the plant species found in forests are thought to have considerable potential value as food and in drugs and medicine. As a resource, forests provide timber for paper, building material, wood panels, sawn lumber, and other wood products. They provide food, and they provide some of the fuelwood that meets the principal energy needs of nearly half the people in the world.

About 60 per cent of the world's forests are in tropical America, Africa and Asia, where most of the large-scale clearance is taking place. Conversion to agriculture is the main cause for the clearance. FAO estimates that 45 per cent of all forests cleared in the tropics are cleared for shifting agriculture. [13] With the growth in population, traditional patterns of shifting agriculture have broken down. A farmer would once have cleared a patch of forest, grown crops until the soil became too poor, and then moved on to a new area, leaving the old area fallow for long enough to build up its fertility and vegetative cover again. Today, however, competition for land makes this method of agriculture almost impossible, and the result is widespread land degradation and deforestation. Almost no tropical forests are intensively managed, and there are few reforestation programmes. Where land is in demand, farmers usually move in when the loggers have left.

The threat to tropical moist forests (TMFs) is now one of the most familiar of all environmental issues. TMFs are the most abundant of all terrestrial habitats, and perform ecological functions that affect vast areas of Latin America, Africa and South East Asia. They cover an area the size of the United States, and contain almost half the world's known animal and plant species. Estimates of the area of TMF being cleared annually vary from about six million hectares to 20 million hectares (15 to 50 million acres). In countries where land is scarce, TMFs are often seen as wasteland that has to be cleared and converted to more economically 'useful' pursuits. Conversion to agriculture is particularly widespread in heavily populated TMF countries, such as Indonesia. Agriculture brings in its wake new roads and settlements, which in turn cause more forest to be cleared.

Timber harvesting is a major cause of Third World forest clearance. Although harvesting for export contributes relatively little to total TMF clearance, the proportion varies from country to country, and in some cases is growing. Almost half of all cut tropical hardwood is exported, of which one-third goes to Europe. Demand from the North for tropical hardwoods as a whole grew particularly after 1950, with European imports increasing nine-fold between 1950 and 1973 alone, and 19-fold in Japan. Demand for industrial hardwood in tropical regions has meanwhile grown just 2.5 times.[14] FAO predicts that production of tropical hardwoods will double by the end of the century. About 40 per cent will be imported by the North. Most of Europe's hardwood comes from the three areas facing the severest deforestation: West Africa, Central Africa, and South East Asia. According to Jack Westoby, a forester formerly with FAO, Northern foresters log Southern forests mainly because the wood is cheaper, there being no compulsion for them to meet the bill of renewing or replacing the forest they have removed.[15]

Britain's record in hardwood consumption is better than many of its Northern neighbours. Hardwood constitutes only 7.5 per cent of total timber imports, and the amount of hardwood imported has fallen from nearly 1.4 million cubic metres in 1964 to 686,000 cubic metres in 1982 – largely because of declining demand for wood in construction. But the main tropical sources of British timber imports include major TMF countries such as Brazil, Malaysia and Indonesia. Imports of tropical timber amounted to nearly one-sixth of all UK timber imports in 1982. British imports from Malaysia in 1982 were 239,000 cubic metres, or about 7 per cent of Malaysia's total timber exports. This may be a small proportion, but the Malaysian timber industry – the most developed of almost any TMF country – has taken a particularly heavy toll of the country's tropical rain forests. At the time of independence in 1957, 74 per cent of peninsular Malaysia was forested. By 1977, the figure was 55 per cent, due very largely to timber harvesting.[16]

New Scientist reported in March 1983 that the British timber industry was becoming increasingly worried that public concern about TMF destruction could harm its business.[17]

Logging takes its toll of all forests. FAO estimates that 210 million hectares (520 million acres) of closed forest (forests dense enough to prevent appreciable growth of grass) have been opened to logging so far, and virgin forest is being opened at a rate of 4.4 million hectares (10.9 million acres) every year. Commercial logging is very selective, with only the most valuable hardwoods cut, but this is usually enough to destroy much of the surrounding woodland and vegetation.

Conversion to cattle ranching is one particular reason for TMF clearance in which the North – particularly the United States – appears to have a hand. Growing demand for beef has encouraged many Latin American countries to convert forest into cattle ranches. Ranching accounted for 38 per cent of all deforestation in Brazil between 1966 and 1975, and more than one-quarter of Central America's forests have been converted since 1960. According to Norman Myers, nearly all the beef produced by six Central American countries has gone to the United States – the 'hamburger connection'.[18]

It is difficult to say how far Britain is implicated in its own 'hamburger connection'. About 85 per cent of the unprocessed beef eaten in Britain is home produced, and another 12 per cent comes from the EEC. Britain imports beef from only two Latin American countries – Brazil and Uruguay – which together supply just over 2 per cent of British needs. Much of this Latin American beef is high grade (and so unlikely to be used in hamburgers) and comes from long-established ranches (which have not therefore contributed to the recent acceleration of TMF clearance). Hamburgers account for just over 5 per cent of British beef consumption. Even if all the beef imported from Brazil was used in hamburgers it would still only account for less than one-third of the content.[19] However, the position may yet change. Consumption of hamburgers in this country is projected to grow by more than one-third by 1990, and Brazil has long fostered the ambition of becoming the world's largest beef exporter and capitalizing on the projected growth in world demand.

In the North, forests face different threats, mainly from over-consumption, the conversion of natural woodland, and acid rain. According to Global 2000, forest is one of the few major natural resources in which Europe can expect to remain reasonably self-sufficient, even though it has only 3.5 per cent of the world's forest cover. But one of the prices being paid to ensure more efficient management and greater production is that natural forest throughout Europe is being replaced with younger and less diverse commercial plantations. The effect of this is to remove natural woodland ecosystems and habitats. The area of forest in Europe is projected to grow, but only because of the spread of commercial forest.

The North as a whole is three times richer in forest resources per capita than the South,[20] but its consumption of timber and wood products is high, and rising. The average European, for example, uses 120 kg (265 lbs) of paper and board per year. The average Indian uses just 2 kg (4.4 lbs). One European uses as much wood as 40 people in the Third World.

While the South consumes nearly 90 per cent of its wood as fuel, the North consumes 90 per cent of the world's processed forest products. More than one-third of the world's annual commercial wood harvest is turned into paper. By the end of the century, the share could be closer to one-half. Paper is crucial to the growth of communication: computer print-outs, letters, reports, facsimile transmission, telexes, newspapers, magazines, packaging, etc. The EEC has to import 29 per cent of its paper and board and 63 per cent of its woodpulp. The UK alone consumes 7 per cent of the world's newsprint, and has to import over 78 per cent of its needs (compared to 50 per cent in 1969). In 1983, 61 per cent of the UK's paper and board needs were imported. Total consumption was seven million tonnes, higher than any European country except West Germany.

No one is yet really certain of the likely long-term effects of acid rain on forests, but nearly one-third of West Germany's forests (2.3 million hectares or 5.7 million acres) were found to be damaged by acid rain in

1983, and another million hectares (2.5 million acres) in Poland and Czechoslovakia. A report in February 1984 from the National Swedish Board of Forestry revealed that 244 stands of forest in southern Sweden were damaged. In more than half, every tenth tree was damaged or dying. Local forestry advisers pointed to air pollution from abroad as the cause. [21]

ENERGY

The world depends on fossil fuels for 96 per cent of its energy needs: oil for 44 per cent, coal for 31 per cent and natural gas for 21 per cent. Few countries are self-sufficient in any of these fuels. In some developing countries, notably India, Bangladesh and Tanzania, the cost of oil imports is more than half the total export earnings. The rise of oil has been recent. In 1950, oil supplied less than 30 per cent of the world's commercial energy. In the next 23 years, oil extraction increased by 400 per cent [22] and world oil consumption grew at 7 per cent annually. If consumption had continued at the same rate after the energy crisis of 1973-74 (when the oil price jumped by 260 per cent), we would today be using nearly twice as much oil as in 1973, and known reserves could well have been used up by 1990. [23] OPEC may have been unpopular at the time for raising oil prices, but it forced the world to conserve a valuable resource. The oil price rises of the 1970s have resulted in almost no growth in annual oil consumption – 20.5 billion barrels in 1983 compared with 20.4 billion in 1973 (there was a peak of 23.8 billion in 1979). Oil provides a prime example of how demand for a resource has been contained by drastically increasing the cost of supply and how as a result the overall standard of living has been very little affected. Per capita oil consumption today – 4.4 barrels (700 litres or 154 gallons) – is lower than at any time since the late 1960s. There has been a 14 per cent fall in world oil consumption since 1979: the result of using all energy more efficiently and of substituting other energy sources for oil.

The countries with the best records in reducing oil consumption are the largest consumers: the industrialized countries of the North which consume more than 60 per cent of the world's oil but produce only 25 per cent. After peaking in the 1970s, Britain, the US, France, West Germany and Japan have all cut oil consumption. In the South, the story varies. Brazil has one of the most advanced fuel alcohol schemes in the world, and in the period 1979-81 alone reduced its oil consumption by

10 per cent. However, in the same period, Mexico more than doubled its consumption.

The fact that global oil consumption is down should not make us blind to the problems that remain unresolved. While it is true that the consumption of refined oil products in the UK fell by nearly 29 per cent between 1972 and 1982, this was achieved mainly by reductions in the consumption of fuel oil (down 60 per cent) and diesel (down 20 per cent). These figures disguise the fact that petrol consumption has in fact *risen* by 40 per cent. Britons now use 377 litres (83 gallons) of petrol per person per year, compared with only 273 litres (60 gallons) in 1972. The average consumption per car has risen 12 per cent. This has been despite petrol price rises and the advent of more fuel-efficient cars. While Canada and the United States are expected to have reduced petrol use between 1978 and 1985 by 34 per cent, and Australia by 28 per cent, the UK will achieve an overall reduction of only 9 per cent.

Although oil mainly comprises carbon and hydrogen, it also contains a variety of highly complex molecular structures. It is rich in compounds and organic materials which have properties and ingredients of considerable potential use in many other fields (notably medicine). Simply burning it is wasting much of its potential. Oil is a limited and effectively irreplaceable resource – because it was formed over a period of millions of years. At some stage in the future it must inevitably run out. Between 1976 and 1981, the world's known reserves fell by more than 10 per cent, and oil is now being used up faster than new stocks are being found. When it remains only in limited quantities that makes it expensive to extract, people are likely to be highly critical of the manner in which it was squandered in the twentieth century.

Oil spills continue to kill tens of thousands of sea birds, disrupt coastal fisheries, and foul beaches and coastlines. Six months after the 1978 Amoco Cadiz disaster, a study showed that 30 per cent of local fauna and 5 per cent of the flora had been destroyed. Low-income fishermen in the South have had their livelihoods undermined for months at a time by the effects of oil spills. UNEP reports that shipping accounts for less than half the oil spilled at sea – and only 10 per cent of that comes from tanker accidents.[24] But oil slicks are frequently reported along main tanker routes, particularly the Red Sea, the Straits of Malacca (between Malaysia and Indonesia), the Mediterranean, the Caribbean and the South China Sea. North Sea oil fields bring the ever-present danger of

THE INTERNATIONAL ENVIRONMENT

spills closer to home – even though it is not a main tanker route. The UK's northern North Sea sector alone had 25 offshore oilfields in production and seven under development at the beginning of 1984.[25] Oil spill contingency planning is improving, but accidents do occur. In 1978, more than 500 spills and five major incidents (including Amoco Cadiz) were reported off the UK. Over 10,000 birds died as a result. Fish, marine mammals such as seals and entire marine food chains were also affected.

One relatively small incident illustrates the dangers. In December 1978, the 193,000-tonne vessel Esso Bernicia was entering Sullom Voe in the Shetlands when a mechanical failure on one of the tugs pulling the tanker compelled the tug to slip its tow line. It got in the way of another tug, whose tow line snapped. The tanker drifted and crashed into a nearby jetty three times, putting a gash in its side through which 1,170 tons of oil were spilled. Booms failed to contain the oil, and the pollution spread. The spilled oil took several weeks and £2.5 million to clean up – but not before 3,700 sea birds (made up of 49 species) had died. The first deaths of otters from oil spills were also recorded.[26]

Another worrying development is the interest being shown in drilling for oil in Antarctica. No oil has yet been found there, but there are strong indications that it exists.[27] If it is found and exploited, then the threat of spills, tanker accidents and blow-outs will follow. Oil pollution could have a serious effect on Antarctic marine and bird life.

POLLUTION

Pollution was one of the earliest environmental issues to attract widespread public condemnation, and one of the first to generate corrective legislation. But while some forms of pollution have been limited and controlled, others have become worse, and new forms have emerged with implications beyond national frontiers.

Transnational pollution has been given new meaning in the past 20 years with the advent of acid deposition, more commonly known as acid rain. When coal and oil are burned, they release sulphur and nitrogen into the atmosphere as gaseous oxides. The coal burned in coal-fired power stations, and the petrol and oil used in road vehicles, are the sources of 90 per cent of atmospheric sulphur in the industrial regions of North America and Europe. Some of the sulphur and nitrogen is absorbed by vegetation, but much mixes with moisture in the atmosphere, forming

81

sulphuric and nitric acids. The exact process is still open to debate, but it appears that, when this moisture forms into droplets, it falls as acidic rain. Carbonic acid is naturally present in rainwater, and some acidity in rain is useful in helping to break down nutrients in the soil. But rain that is too acid increases the acidity of lakes, rivers and soils, and attacks plant life.

Because the oxidized moisture can travel hundreds of kilometres before falling as rain, the areas that cause the pollution rarely suffer the worst effects. The prevailing winds in the northern hemisphere blow much of the acid moisture northwards, so sulphur and nitrogen emitted by factories in England may fall as acid rain in Scotland, Norway or Sweden, and that emitted by factories in the United States may fall as acid rain in Canada. On the pH scale, a reading of 7.0 is neutral; the lower the reading, the more acid is present. The rain that fell in pre-industrial times was thought to have a slightly acidic pH of about 5.6. The average drop of rain falling in parts of Europe and North America today is between 4.0 and 5.0. But the pH drops markedly in industrial areas.

Since 1950, sulphur dioxide emissions have doubled and sulphur concentrations in rainfall have increased by half in parts of Europe. Seven countries now account for 90 per cent of the total output of European sulphur. The largest is the UK, followed by Italy, Poland, East Germany, France, West Germany and Czechoslovakia. The effects have been many and widespread. In Sweden, about 20,000 lakes (20 per cent of the country's total) have been acidified. (Lakes killed by acid become sparklingly clear because their water is no longer clouded by organic life.) Fish have died in half the lakes in the Canadian province of Ontario. The number of salmon and trout in Norwegian rivers has greatly declined. Forests are major victims, with trees losing their vitality and becoming more susceptible to injury. In many countries, buildings are literally dissolving: for example, the hieroglyphics on the west side – the side against which rain is most often blown by the wind – of Cleopatra's Needle in New York are almost indecipherable, while those on the sheltered east side are still clear.[28] In Poland's industrial belt in recent years, railway tracks have been so corroded that trains cannot travel at more than 40 kph (25 mph). Acid rain has been recorded in the Arctic and in the industrial areas of China, Brazil, India, Zambia and South Africa.

In July 1984, the West German coalition government was threatened by the opposition of the Free Democrats, the junior partners in the coalition government, to plans to allow a new coal-fired power station to operate without emission filters. Only the year before, the Bundestag had passed legislation aimed at reducing sulphur emissions by one-third in ten years. The new plant, at Buschhaus in Lower Saxony, was not due to be fitted with filters until 1987. By then it would have emitted 125,000 tonnes of sulphur.[29]

A recent report from the Organization for Economic Cooperation and Development (OECD) estimates that acid rain is costing the EEC between £33 and £44 billion annually. Some governments try liming lakes to offset the acidity; this is not only expensive but is treating the symptoms rather than the causes, and shifting responsibility for corrective action from the polluters to the polluted.

The amount of coal burned in Europe is forecast to increase by 50 per cent in the next 20 years. This will result in a rise of one-third in sulphur depositions unless controlling measures are taken. The technology already exists for Britain, the biggest producer of sulphur emissions in Europe, to decrease its emissions by up to one-third during that period. Combustion gas desulphurization equipment could be installed in power stations, or fuel oil could be desulphurized at refineries.[30]

The three major stumbling blocks to any action being taken in Britain are first that the effects of acid rain are not well known in this country, second that there has been little effective pressure from Europe for us to do anything, and third that both the government and nationalized industries are far from convinced about the causes of acid rain. In June 1984, a Department of Energy report suggested that destruction ascribed to acid rain was actually the fault of ozone, and that less than 2 per cent of air pollution over Norway and Sweden came from Britain.[31]

The National Coal Board argues that sulphur emissions in Britain have been falling steadily since 1973 and are now at 1940 levels. The Central Electricity Generating Board (CEGB) could install scrubbers in its power stations, thus screening off sulphur, but until recently insisted that the connection between fossil fuel-burning and acid rain had not been proved. As recently as 1983, the Board was saying that reducing sulphur dioxide emissions from power stations would have little effect on reducing acid rain.[32] In 1984, the National Coal Board and the CEGB launched a five-year £5 million project to look into acid rain. This angered Scandinavian scientists who said that most of the basic research had already been carried out, and that Britain was simply buying time. In February 1984, the Royal Commission on Environmental Pollution called for more spending on anti-pollution measures, and argued that control of pollution 'is not an optional extra. It is a fundamental component of national economic and social policy, and has many international implications'.[33] Only recently has the British government felt any need to look seriously at the acid rain problem in order to improve relations with other countries within the EEC.

West Germany, after years of being condemned as the arch-polluter of Europe, was encouraged to take action against pollution because of the country's dying forests in 1983, and is now a supporter of measures against acid rain. West Germany's action has confirmed Britain's position on acid rain as the worst in Europe. The Scandinavians are united in their condemnation, but have been able to exert little effective pressure for change. Britain, like West Germany, may finally be moved to action by the effects of acid rain within its own borders. Rain falling in Pitlochry, Scotland, as long ago as 1974 had a pH of 2.4 (more acidic than vinegar). Fish in many Welsh rivers are dying. Buildings in London and Birmingham are dissolving: an inch of Portland stone has gone from the surface of St Paul's Cathedral. Acid rain may be cutting crop yields in Britain by as much as 10 per cent, costing British farmers £200 million annually.[34] And ironically the effects of acid rain on Scandinavian forests have serious implications for British timber demand.

Coal-burning power stations account for 63 per cent of sulphur dioxide emissions and 46 per cent of nitrogen oxide emissions in the UK.[35] Reducing the amount of sulphur emitted by installing scrubbers in chimneys or by using desulphurized fuel is one way of curbing acid rain. But this will take time and money. Another, quicker, way is through reducing demand for electricity. British domestic consumers account for 39 per cent of national electricity demand. The second largest source of nitrogen oxide – 28 per cent of the total – is road traffic. As the amount of traffic on British roads increases, so does the amount of nitrogen oxide in the atmosphere. Four out of every five vehicles on British roads are private cars. If people were to use them less, and public transport more, nitrogen oxide emissions would fall.

The profligate use of fossil fuels implicates consumers in a second major pollution issue: the build-up of carbon dioxide (CO_2) in the atmosphere. Although there is still much uncertainty about the consequences, there has been a proven build-up of atmospheric CO_2 – by an estimated 15 to 25 per cent since 1860. The source of the build-up is thought to be the burning of fossil fuels, which releases the carbon in the fuels. Forests and oceans absorb some of this but, since the beginning of the nineteenth century particularly, the amount of CO_2 remaining in the atmosphere has grown. If coal and oil were to continue to be used at their present rates, the concentration of carbon dioxide in the atmosphere could double over the next 45 years.[36]

The atmosphere acts like glass in a greenhouse: heat is trapped from the sun, creating conditions necessary for life and growth. About 35 to 50 per cent is reflected back into space; 10 to 20 per cent is absorbed by the atmosphere; and 45 to 50 per cent reaches the surface of the earth. If all solar heat was reflected back into space, the earth would be too cold to support life. If all solar heat was absorbed, on the other hand, the earth would be too hot. So some absorption is desirable – without this 'greenhouse effect' there would be no life on earth.

The build-up of CO_2 has had the effect of reducing the amount of solar heat reflected back into space. Before about 1950, the main cause of this was the removal of the forest cover that absorbs CO_2. Since then, the burning of fossil fuels has been making a bigger contribution. The net long-term result could be to raise global temperatures. Current estimates are that a doubling of CO_2 concentrations could raise average temperatures around the world by 2 to 3°C. It took a temperature rise of only 4°C to bring the earth out of the last ice age 11,000 years ago. A further rise now could have several serious effects. It could alter wind, rainfall and oceanic circulation patterns. It could disrupt ecosystems and life-cycles by causing a shift in high-rainfall zones. It could move the world's crop-growing regions further north, away from the grain belts of North America. Most extreme of all, some scientists argue that a melting of the polar ice caps would not be impossible. If this happened, there would be a rise in the level of the world's oceans of up to 5 metres (16 feet), which would put most low-lying coastal areas under water. There is no certainty yet that the build-up of atmospheric carbon dioxide is causing a warming of the earth. But just the threat has been enough to encourage an ambitious UN research programme, and active monitoring of carbon dioxide trends by numerous agencies.

WILDLIFE

The plight of wildlife probably elicits more sympathy than any other environmental issue. Britons alone annually give millions of pounds to wildlife conservation charities. Well-meaning campaigns are launched to save pandas from extinction, to call off the Canadian seal cull, to stop whaling, and so on. But while money and technical assistance may ease the problem, they will rarely help tackle the basic causes, many of which are rooted in demand for resources, and hence in the way we live. For more than two-thirds of the earth's threatened species the major problem is habitat destruction. No amount of protection aimed at individual species alone is going to save them as long as the indirect threats remain. While giving money to wildlife charities with one hand, most of us daily do something that is guaranteed to make our donation completely useless:

· Throwing away waste paper instead of recycling it contributes to the destruction of natural woodland, the habitat of many of the world's most threatened species. Plants, in particular, are threatened in this way.

· Increasing road traffic contributes to the generation of atmospheric sulphur dioxide (which falls as acid rain that kills forests, fish and plant life in Northern Europe); ensures that more land is paved over with roads; and ensures that offshore oil drilling in the North Sea is maintained, heightening the danger of oil spills which annually kill thousands of sea birds.

· The over-consumption and waste of food encourages the conversion of more land to agriculture, the use of pesticides in the interests of greater production, and the over-exploitation of fisheries. It also reduces wildlife habitat. Nowhere is this more visible than in the UK, where, in the interests of greater efficiency and bigger profits, farmers clear hedgerows to turn small fields into big ones and 'reclaim' marginal land on moors, downs and in wetlands.

Moderating pressure of this kind is a far more effective means to successful conservation than trying to cure the problems that arise as a consequence. Sympathy and charity have their place, but can often be misdirected. Two particular issues – international trade in wildlife and wildlife products, and the question of wild genetic resources – illustrate some of the consequences of demand and supply, and the urgency of conserving wildlife more effectively.

International trade in wildlife

Wildlife and wildlife products were among the first commodities to be traded by humans. Primitive societies exchanged animal furs; fashion vogues in Europe created a demand for bird plumage and other products; Victorian naturalists exchanged specimens; and society today makes big business out of international trade in furs, ivory, rhino horn and other products. It was estimated that the value of international trade in wildlife in 1984 was $2.5 billion.[37] Hunting and direct trade have between them accounted for the extinction and threatened extinction of mammals, birds, reptiles, amphibians and plants alike. The elephant, rhino and tiger, and species of crocodile, turtle, whale and seal have all had their numbers seriously reduced by trade demands.

International trade in wildlife was one of the earliest topics on the agenda of IUCN, and active campaigning during the 1960s and 1970s led to the coming into force in 1979 of the Convention on International Trade in Endangered Species (CITES). So far 86 countries have signed, agreeing to regulate trade in more than 600 species listed in three appendices. The passage of CITES and the publicity given to wildlife trade by conservation groups since the 1960s has had the effect of stifling the vogue for wearing, collecting or displaying wildlife products, but considerable demand remains none the less. Illicit trade and difficulties in enforcing CITES have combined to ensure continuing trade, for example, in ivory and rhino horn. Demand for the latter, used particularly for dagger handles in North Yemen, has helped reduce world rhino numbers by 70 per cent since 1970.[38]

The South is a net producer of wildlife products and the North a net consumer. According to TRAFFIC-US, a wildlife trade watchdog group, the United States accounts for about one-third of the global wildlife market, and Japan and Western Europe for most of the balance.[39] Wildlife products (furs, skins, horns, etc) rather than live animals make up most of the trade, notable exceptions being birds and animals used in medical research. Despite growing opposition, four million animals are used every year in British laboratory experiments. The war against poliomyelitis has so far cost the lives of 1.5 million monkeys. At the height of the campaign in the 1950s, nearly 5,000 monkeys were being flown into Britain every week. Monkeys have been used in medical research, but they have also been used in simulated car crashes, in freezing experiments, and to test the effects of radiation and neutron bombs. This despite the fact that all 184 primates are included in the CITES appendices.

At a 1982 London conference reported by *New Scientist*, academics and scientists from the UK's major research institutes agreed that the number of experiments on live animals could be cut by half almost overnight if the government and the civil servants who regulated the marketing of drugs were more flexible and if the results of tests were shared more widely.[40] Tissue cultures could be used to pre-screen new drugs and chemicals. Anti-vivisectionists argue that a reduction in the number of new and non-essential drugs coming on to the market would make a big difference. They might also argue that decreased demand for these drugs would make a difference.

Genetic resources

One of the most serious problems posed by the destruction of nature, and one that has universal implications, is the threat to wild genetic resources: the characteristics of wild plants or animals that are of actual or potential use to people. All species of commercial fruit, vegetables and livestock were once wild. Market demands for ready and reliable supplies have since dictated the species that have been domesticated and most widely cultivated. Very few people in industrial societies now eat wild food. Yet the quality and continued supply of commercial food is often the result of improvements made by interbreeding with wild species. Robert and Christine Prescott-Allen cite many examples of these improvements in their book *Genes from the Wild*.[41]

According to one plant geneticist, the tomato could not be grown at all as a commercial crop without the help of its wild relatives. Interbreeding with wild tomatoes has made domesticated tomatoes more nutritious and has enabled them to be grown all the year round, making them one of the world's most widely eaten vegetables. But the desire to meet consumer demand can have bad effects. Most commercial tomatoes have been bred to have a healthy red colour and firm skins, but have thereby lost their taste. Each stage in their breeding has taken them further and further from their wild state. Wild tomatoes may look dull and will bruise easily, but they taste much better than their commercial relatives. Commercial potatoes have had a similar fate. They look and taste much the same, yet their wild Latin American relatives come in a variety of shapes, colours, textures and tastes. There are 154 species of wild potato, but we mainly eat only three cultivated varieties: Arran Pilot, Majestic and King Edward.

Interbreeding has produced food crops resistant to disease, higher yields, vigour, and other characteristics, without which human eating habits would be very different. Wheat, rice, maize and barley, for instance, which make up 90 per cent of the world's annual grain production, have all been improved with the help of wild genetic resources, particularly for disease resistance. When the potato was first introduced to Europe in the sixteenth century, only two species were grown, making them highly vulnerable to disease. (This was proved in the late blight epidemic of 1845-46 which resulted in widespread tragedy with the Irish famine.) Since then, new wild species of potato have been imported and bred with domesticated species to give them a degree of disease resistance that would make epidemics very unlikely.

The sunflower is currently the world's second largest source of plant oil, thanks entirely to interbreeding of wild and domesticated species. In the late nineteenth century, the insect pest *Phylloxera vitifoliae* all but destroyed the vineyards of France, Spain, Germany, Italy and other wine-producing countries. Wild vines with resistance to *Phylloxera* were imported from North America and now form the basis of all the vines grown in the *Phylloxera*-contaminated areas. According to one scientist, without its wild relatives there would probably be no viable sugarcane industry at all. Wild sugarcane has given domesticated species a vigour and resistance to disease that has helped more than double the yield of sugar and has made it possible to grow sugarcane in areas that could not otherwise have grown it commercially.

The examples continue, and the potential – for crop foods, timber, fish and livestock – is enormous. So is the potential for new crops altogether from the wild. Most people, wherever they live, rely on a very limited range of food crops. The average British household relies on about 30 main food crops for most of its grain, cereal and vegetable needs. Most British kitchens have the same staples: potatoes, tomatoes, peas, carrots, cabbage, lettuce, cucumber, etc. More adventurous cooks might have graduated to pulses and started dabbling in some of the more exotic vegetables and fruits stocked by some stores in Britain: sweet potatoes, alfalfa, yams, kiwi fruit, pawpaw, etc. Others might have experimented with new species on holiday, such as mangosteens, durian, etc.

But this is just the tip of the iceberg. Not only are there many more kinds of fruit and vegetable already in use in other countries, but there are thousands of potentially edible species of which we know little or nothing. Some of these may be crucial in helping to ease the world food shortage; others may be able to survive in arid or cold regions; others may have useful medicinal properties; others may offer new trading opportunities for poor countries; yet others may have useful characteristics for interbreeding with cultivated crops. And they are not limited only to tropical regions, but can be found on our own doorstep. For instance, edible berries, wild fruit, food plants and herbs grow in abundance in hedgerows, meadows, fields, and woods all over Britain.

Unfortunately, this stock of wild genes is being gradually whittled away. Wild genetic resources face the same threats as all wild species. Species that are found only in limited areas face particular problems. The two main habitats of the 154 species of wild potato for example are central Mexico and the central Andes. Several sunflower species are threatened, and at least one Californian species is probably extinct. Wild species of tomato, chickpea, banana, citrus fruits, nuts, sugarcane, and coffee all face varying threats. Timber species too are threatened. The Prescott-Allens give the example of the tarout cypress, a drought-resistant and frost-tolerant tree that produces timber with a wide variety of uses. It has been cut down so much for firewood that it is now restricted to a 200 sq km area in eastern Algeria. Only 153 living trees are known to exist.

Wild relatives of domestic livestock are also threatened. Over-hunting, habitat destruction and competition from introduced species has led to all four wild cattle species, two out of six wild sheep species, one out of four pig species, three out of six goat species, and five out of seven horse species being classified as threatened.

TOURISM

Tourism can provide a country or community with a major source of income and employment, revitalize local industries, and give a boost to the preservation and restoration of cultural and natural resources. Yet it can also be one of the most destructive forms of exploitation of the citizens and resources of one country by the citizens of another. Between 1970 and 1980, the annual number of tourist arrivals in the world rose from 180 million to 286 million. While this benefited many areas, many others were approaching the limits of desirable tourist influx. The 1980 World Tourism Conference in Manila issued a declaration to the effect that the obvious economic advantages of tourism needed to be balanced with the need to conserve the heritage of the host countries. Tourism only helps a country if it benefits the majority of people, and is not run at the expense of the physical and cultural environment.

The biggest travelling nations are the United States (with 14.7 per cent of traffic), West Germany and France. The UK comes fourth (6.5 per cent of traffic). In 1980, Europeans accounted for 72.8 per cent of all international tourist traffic. The amount spent by tourists (excluding fares) rose from $18.2 billion in 1970 to $92 billion in 1980. For countries such as Kenya, Malaysia, Morocco, Malta, Tunisia and much of the West Indies, this represents a major economic boon. In Bermuda, tourism provides for three-quarters of all the jobs. But many of the profits of tourism never even reach the countries visited. Much of the income from tourism goes to buying the goods and services used by tourists; some is the profit made by international hotel groups; and some goes to travel agents and to promotion and publicity abroad.

Nepal provides a prime example. In 1982, about 162,000 tourists visited the country, many to go trekking in the Himalayas. The walk to the Everest base camp is now so popular that at the height of the tourist season there are more tourists than local residents in the Everest region. Mountaineers have over the years left a trail of garbage and discarded equipment. Tourism earned Nepal about $50 million in foreign exchange in 1982, but it spent $35 million importing goods and services for the tourists, and the remaining $15 million went to travel agencies and hotel groups. Tourism has also brought inflation, pushing the prices of many staple foods beyond the reach of local people.[42]

Lakes, mountains, oceans, national parks and reserves, wilderness and unspoiled countryside hold the strongest attraction for tourists. The value of tourism can often ensure that these areas are preserved, and that conservation is seen as a justifiable form of land use. The local environment can benefit; a tourist development project at Ixtapa in Mexico for example has brought the nearby town water supplies, a sewage system, paved roads, tree-planting and coastal protection measures.[43]

But there are many drawbacks. Wilderness and unspoiled coasts are invaded by roads, hotels, shops, and restaurants. Coral reefs can be excavated or dynamited to provide building material or to make way for marinas and harbours. Historic cities and villages can become clogged with traffic, bringing noise and air pollution. A recent study in Malaysia[44] showed how investment that might have been used to provide local people with better facilities was being channelled into providing tourists with better utilities, transport, shelter and recreation. Seven beach hotels on Penang Island were consuming 17 per cent of the island's electricity, or 36 times more per head than local people. Pollution from human waste was worst in the sea in front of the hotels. The best beaches were out of bounds to local people, whose culture and values were also being eroded by visitors. While many local people went without clean water and adequate sanitation, the hotels had the best possible amenities. And while the tourist trade earns Malaysia $800 million per year, much of the money spent by tourists is used to buy imported food, drink and consumer items.

Thailand is a country whose values have been warped by tourism. In 1983, it earned about $1 billion from tourism (enough to pay all the interest on its overseas debt), but much of its tourist trade depends on bar girls, massage parlours and prostitution. An estimated 40 per cent of women in Bangkok earn their living through prostitution. Although they earn higher salaries than they might in other jobs, prostitution is encouraging crime, drug addiction and venereal disease. As many as three million Thais may be suffering some form of sexually transmitted disease.[45]

The souvenir trade at one time accounted for a considerable proportion of wildlife destruction. As recently as the early 1970s, visitors to Kenya could buy side tables made from elephant feet, drums made from zebra skin, carpets made from the skins of colobus monkeys, wallets made from rhino hide, elephant hair bracelets and fly whisks, and table lamps made from helmet shells. Tourists to countries such as Zambia are still known to be offered black market rhino horn. Trade in most wildlife species is now either banned or discouraged in most countries, but visitors to many coastal resorts can still freely buy shells and corals taken from nearby reefs. The biggest beach hotel in Bali, Indonesia, sits opposite a reef now barren of almost all life, a direct result of the tourist trade.

One recent victim of the wildlife trade is the giant clam. It lives in shallow waters, making it accessible to divers, and in countries such as Tonga and Papua New Guinea is a major source of food. The Japanese regard the meat of clams as a delicacy. Their shells are sold to tourists and residents alike in many Pacific and Indian Ocean states to be used as anything from table lamps to bird baths, wash basins and floor tiles. The severe over-exploitation they suffer is beginning to pose a severe threat to their existence.[46]

INTERNATIONAL ENVIRONMENTAL ORGANIZATIONS

International environmental problems need international solutions. The founding of a postwar rash of international organizations included several environmental conservation and management bodies. Natural resources were on the agenda of some of the specialized UN agencies set up immediately after the Second World War, notably the Rome-based Food and Agriculture Organization (FAO), which looked at the management of food and forestry resources as part of the plan of post-war reconstruction. Since then, it has become increasingly involved in environment and resource questions, particularly in as much as they relate to food, forestry and agriculture. UNESCO turned its attention to conservation briefly, following its creation in 1946, but only because of the personal interest of its Director-General, Julian Huxley. It has since played only a peripheral role, although it collaborated on the World Conservation Strategy and is the sponsor of the Man and the Biosphere programme (MAB), launched in 1971 to promote the declaration of a network of reserves representing the world's major ecosystem types. Among the UK's biosphere reserves are Braunton Burrows in North Devon and Beinn Eighe in Scotland.

The United Nations Environment Programme (UNEP), with headquarters in Nairobi, monitors the environmental policies of all UN agencies. UNEP has no executive powers, has constant budget problems, has to keep itself involved in many activities and concerns, and is torn between the conflicting priorities of North and South.

For all this, UNEP has succeeded in increasing the level of awareness in the environment among UN agencies, and has brought governments together to discuss shared resource problems. Its most notable success is the Regional Seas Programme, where UNEP has brought together governments (some with very different political views) to agree on joint management of their shared regional seas. The most advanced programme so far is the Mediterranean Action Plan, involving 16 countries. Several pieces of legislation on pollution have been agreed, and 84 national laboratories are now involved in a co-operative monitoring and research programme.

A notable UNEP failure is its anti-desertification programme. Entrusted with encouraging the implementation of the Plan of Action drawn up at the 1977 UN Conference on Desertification, UNEP has been unable (often through no fault of its own) to encourage affected nations to act, or to encourage the aid donors of the North to finance anti-desertification measures.

Outside the United Nations, the oldest and most truly international conservation organization is the Swiss-based International Union for Conservation of Nature and Natural Resources (IUCN), whose members include both governments and non-governmental organizations. IUCN's aims were at first limited to nature preservation, but have since broadened to include sustainable development and much wider environmental concerns. Essentially an advisory organization that attempts to influence governments, and to promote conservation action, IUCN is now one of the more active proponents of resolving conflicts between conservation and development.

IUCN was plagued during its early years by a lack of funds, and so set up the World Wildlife Fund (WWF) in 1961 to raise money to finance IUCN projects. WWF has long operated independently, although it shares policy and a headquarters with IUCN. It has affiliated national organizations in 25 countries.

IUCN, UNEP and WWF are now regarded as the three key international environmental organizations, particularly since their joint launch in 1980 of the World Conservation Strategy. Outside this triumvirate there are few truly global organizations, although global problems are on the agenda of campaigning groups such as Friends of the Earth and Greenpeace (see pages 33-4). The Washington DC-based Worldwatch Institute analyses global problems and publishes a very useful series of papers on key topics. The International Institute for Environment and Development (IIED), based in London and Washington DC, carries out research into the conflicting demands of development and environmental management. Numerous organizations with regional interests also exist. In Europe, the European Environmental Bureau, an umbrella group that comprises about 60 non-governmental organizations (NGOs) and monitors EEC activities, is the most influential.

REFERENCES

1 World Development Movement (1979) *The Tea Trade*. London
2 Independent Commission on International Development Issues (1980) *North-South: A Programme for Survival*. Pan, London
3 Ibid
4 Eckholm, Erik (1982) *Down to Earth*. Pluto Press, London
5 Scherr, Jacob (1982) *Hazardous Exports: A New International Order?* Earthscan, London
6 Madeley, John (1983) *The Cigarette's Last Frontier*. Earthscan, London
7 IIED (1982) *Annual Report 1981-82*. IIED, London
8 World Bank (1979) *Environment and Development*. World Bank, Washington DC
9 Chauhan, Sumi Krishna (1982) *Parks versus People*. Earthscan, London
10 World Bank (1984) *World Development Report*. Washington DC
11 Ward, Barbara (1982) Foreword to Eckholm, Erik *op cit*
12 *The Global 2000 Report to the President* (1982). Penguin, Harmondsworth
13 FAO (1982) *Tropical Forest Resources*. Forestry Paper 30, Rome
14 Pringle, S L (1976) Tropical moist forests in world demand, supply and trade. In *Unasylva*, Nos 112-113
15 Westoby, Jack (1983) Who's deforesting whom? In *IUCN Bulletin*, Vol 14, No 10-12, October
16 Myers, Norman (1980) *Conversion of Tropical Moist Forests*. National Academy of Sciences, Washington DC
17 Caufield, Catherine (1983) Forest firms fear conservationists' backlash. In *New Scientist*, 24 March
18 Myers, Norman (1979) *The Sinking Ark*. Pergamon, Oxford
19 Based on figures supplied by the Ministry of Agriculture, Fisheries and Food, and the Meat and Livestock Commission
20 Global 2000 *op cit*
21 Svensson, Gert (1984) Forest at risk? In *Acid Magazine*, Spring

22 Deudley, D and Flavin, C (1983) *Renewable Energy: The Power to Choose*. W W Norton, New York

23 Brown, Lester *et al* (1984) *State of the World 1984*. W W Norton, New York

24 Holdgate, M W, Kassas, M and White, G F (eds) (1982) *The World Environment 1972-1982*. Tycooly, Dublin

25 Robertson, J G (1984) *The Environmental Impact of North Sea Oil-Related Developments on Scotland*. Habitat Scotland

26 Ibid

27 Mitchell, Barbara (1983) *Frozen Stakes: The Future of Antarctic Minerals*. IIED, London

28 May, John (1982) Dragon's revenge. In *Undercurrents*, No 54

29 *The Times* (1984) 30 July

30 Highton, Nicolas (1982) Controlling the emissions of sulphur compounds in the United Kingdom: Is it worth the cost? In *Ambio*, Vol IX, No 6

31 Department of Energy (1984) *Acidity in the environment*

32 Royal Commission on Environmental Pollution (1984) *Tenth Report*. HMSO, London

33 Ibid

34 Unsworth, Dr Michael (1984) Quoted in *Acid News* No 2, March

35 Royal Commission on Environmental Pollution (1984) *op cit*

36 Gribbin, John (1981) *Carbon Dioxide, Climate and Man*. Earthscan, London

37 Bohlen, Janet (1983) *The United States versus the Wildlife Smugglers*. Earthscan, London

38 Martin, E B and Barzdo, J (1984) The volume of the world's trade in rhino horn. In *Traffic Bulletin*, Vol VI, No I, 11 April

39 Bohlen, Janet (1983) *op cit*

40 *New Scientist* (1982) 4 November

41 Prescott-Allen, Robert and Christine (1983) *Genes from the Wild*. Earthscan, London

42 Bahadur, Shyam (1983) *Sharing the Tourist Dollar*. Earthscan, London

43 Holdgate, Kassas and White *op cit*

44 In *Asian-Pacific Newsletter* (1984), Vol 2, No 1.

45 Smith, Diana (1984) *Sex and Tourism in Thailand*. Earthscan, London

46 de Silva, Donatus (1984) *Clams: The Endangered Giants*. Earthscan, London

ON THE HOME FRONT: THE BRITISH ENVIRONMENT

4

Britain is a small, crowded country. With 56 million people packed into 244,000 sq km (94,250 square miles), demand for land is keen. This demand, allied with Britain's limited resource base and the way land is used, is the quintessential British environmental issue. The factors in the equation are agriculture, urban development and forestry, which respectively account for 79 per cent, 12 per cent and 9 per cent of the UK's land area.

Until the Second World War, Britain's remaining wildlife fitted in reasonably well. Hedgerows, woodlands and marginal land – wetlands, moors and downs which were not economically viable to convert to farming – provided limited but usually adequate wildlife habitats. Wildlife was part of the characteristic landscape of a patchwork quilt of fields and woodland. But the position began to change with the wartime drive to Dig for Victory, which carried over into the postwar years in a programme of intensive and efficient farming. This resulted in alarming inroads being made into what remained of nature. Pressure on land and other resources has been increasing rapidly since the war. Continued demand for housing and transport has encouraged the spread of towns and cities, increased the number of vehicles on the road and multiplied the number of kilometres of road.

At one time, population growth too was an issue. Many of the plans and forecasts used as the basis for postwar planning assumed that the population would grow much faster than it eventually did. The population is now stable, and the UK is one of only 12 countries in the world to have reached zero population growth. With the population no longer growing, it might well be assumed that consumer demand was not growing. In fact, this is not necessarily the case.

AGRICULTURE

British agriculture all but stagnated between the late nineteenth century and the Second World War. But wartime siege conditions changed this. Once the 1942 Committee on Land Utilization in Rural Areas had decided that the aim of British agriculture should be self-sufficiency, the race was on to increase productivity as much as possible within the limited land area available. Almost all the land that could be farmed with available technology was already being farmed, so farmers turned to intensification, the conversion of marginal land and improved yields. Farming went through a technological revolution.

As recently as the late 1940s, farming and conservation were still seen as compatible and harmonious pursuits. Agriculture was seen as a key ingredient in maintaining landscape beauty. But this is no longer so. Farming is now big business, and as Chris Rose notes, the Dan Archer image of the sturdy country farmer has been rapidly dispelled.[1] Grants and other incentives encourage farmers to produce more and more. Estimates of the total annual subsidy paid to British farmers vary from £3.5 billion to £5 billion, or between £175 and £250 for every taxpayer in the country. Marion Shoard's influential *The Theft of the Countryside*, published in 1980, shocked many people with its revelations about the extent to which farmers enjoyed tax benefits, subsidies, rate exemptions and the Common Agricultural Policy Price Support System – all at the expense of the countryside.[2] The demand for 'improved' and 'reclaimed' land for agriculture is the single greatest threat to wildlife and habitats. The drive to make farms more efficient is achieved through bigger farms and fields – hedgerows and woodlands are regarded as obstacles, and are hence cleared. Large parts of the British countryside have been converted into featureless prairie.

The resulting increases in yields have, it is true, been remarkable. Since 1972, while the British population has remained steady and the area under agriculture has actually fallen, production of farm crops (wheat, barley, oats, etc) has risen by nearly 40 per cent, of dairy products by 40 per cent and of fruit and vegetables by 10 per cent. Improved cereal varieties, the increased use of fertilizers, and the widespread switch to winter wheat and barley produced a record harvest in 1984, expected to top the previous record year of 1982 by 10 to 15 per cent. The value of gross product rose from £1.9 billion to £5.4 billion. Yields of wheat rose from 2.85 tonnes per hectare in 1952 to 6.4 tonnes by 1982. Total agricultural production has increased by nearly one-third since the late 1960s. In 1939, Britain imported nearly two-thirds of its food needs. This fell to just over half in 1971 and to 25 per cent in 1983.

However, as David Baldock argues,[3] the remaining shortfall is not necessarily an argument for farmers to produce more. In fact there are at least six good reasons why Britain need not produce more:

1. Agricultural intensification has already done serious and widespread damage to Britain's countryside.
2. Surpluses of temperate foods have already reached crisis proportions in the EEC, giving rise to the most appalling waste as valuable produce is destroyed to maintain market prices.
3. One fact often overlooked is that British agricultural exports are growing. While the value of all UK exports grew by 570 per cent between 1972 and 1982, the value of food and live animal exports (other than processed foods and animal feed) rose by 1,500 per cent. This clearly helps offset the cost of importing food.
4. In his book *Can Britain Feed Itself?*, Kenneth Mellanby argued that Britain could probably become self-sufficient in food if a more moderate (and even more healthy) diet was adopted.[4]
5. Bryn Green points out that 25 per cent of the food produced in Britain is lost to harvesting and processing or thrown out in our domestic garbage, offering a huge potential to meet any production shortfalls.[5]
6. Government planners might do well to realize that home demand for most food is decreasing. While consumption of meats and fruit rose by 2.3 per cent and 7 per cent respectively between 1972 and 1982, consumption of dairy products fell by 10 per cent, vegetables by 3.2 per cent, and bread and flour by 9 per cent.

The drive to self-sufficiency that followed the war became almost a divine cause, and planners made inflated predictions based on the assumption that population and demand would grow rapidly. But population is no longer growing, and demand for many foodstuffs is declining. Britain is still locked into an agricultural ethic that demands increased production and profits at all costs, but a fall in consumer demand must have an effect. Food surpluses are already becoming more and more embarrassing, as the EEC is discovering. Falling demand will add weight to accelerating efforts by the conservation lobby to have farmers agree to a more equitable land use policy. Clearly, a strong agricultural industry is essential to Britain's economy and standard of living, and the aim of self-sufficiency is admirable. But, like all development, to succeed in the long term it must be sustainable. Waste, over-consumption, over-production and the destruction of the countryside make no sense on any terms.

URBAN SPREAD

Urban growth is dwindling throughout the North. In the ten years to 1981, the population of Britain's big urban areas fell overall by 1.9 per cent and that of rural areas grew by 9.7 per cent.[6] People are more mobile; there has been a deliberate policy of expanding new towns; and inner city renewal has not always lived up to its promises. People are moving away from city centres and out to the suburbs or to small towns in rural areas. The biggest changes are taking place in the South West, East Anglia and the East Midlands.

Housing shortages in urban areas are made far worse by the quality of much existing housing. According to the National Federation of Housing Associations, about 1.1 million dwellings are 'unfit' for habitation, 390,000 lack one or more basic amenities, over three million need repairs costing £2,300 or more, and 1.5 million are suffering from major design defects. Changing patterns of demand are adding to the problems. Because the population is moving, demand for existing housing and services is falling and demand for new development is growing.

The first legacy of these changes is that about 15,000 hectares (36,000 acres) of land are every year swallowed up by urban spread: new housing estates, shopping centres, factories, car parks, and all the services needed to maintain a community. The second legacy is the growing area of derelict and wasted land now found in cities. As people move away from inner cities, many hectares of land are left derelict. Commercial and industrial areas become redundant; roads and utilities become underused and neglected; and shopping areas decline. Meanwhile, suburbs edge out into the countryside. The 1982 Survey of Derelict Land reveals that England alone has at least 46,000 hectares (113,000 acres) of derelict land. Some of this is virtually useless, but 34,000 hectares (85,000 acres) are reclaimable. Much of this land is in city areas, and because it is often in areas considered undesirable, builders are unwilling to risk investing in developing it.

Converting old rubbish dumps or disused factory sites into new land for housing or offices not only removes an eyesore from the landscape but reduces the need to build on agricultural land or countryside. The nationalized industries own nearly one-quarter of this derelict land, and are notoriously slow in putting it on to the market. In one recent period of 18 months, only 400 out of 9,700 hectares (1,100 out of 24,000 acres) of the derelict land they own went on the market. City councils also own land, much of it destined to be used to build new council houses. But rate capping and cuts in rate support often mean that this is not possible. Nearly two-thirds of the derelict land suitable for housing in Manchester is owned by the city council which has about 7,800 hectares (19,000 acres) of spare land suitable for development.[7] If all this derelict land were to be developed it would remove much of the need to develop more countryside.

FORESTRY

Forest is a resource with which most European countries are well-endowed. So much so that Europe's forests are expected to meet 80 per cent of increased demand for wood over the next 15 years. But the share of woodland is very unequal, with 37 per cent of European forests in the three Nordic countries. The UK has less than 2 per cent of Europe's total forest area, but is the region's biggest consumer of wood and paper products. Because the UK currently imports 91 per cent of its softwood requirements and nearly two-thirds of its hardwood needs[8] at an annual cost of £2,750 million, it is frequently argued that the country needs commercial forestry to provide more of its own needs. But thanks largely to less waste and more recycling, consumption of wood and paper products in the UK has been falling steadily. In 1980, 46 per cent of British woodpulp supplies came from waste paper. By 1983, the proportion was up to 53 per cent. Between 1972 and 1982, demand for softwood fell by nearly one-quarter, for hardwood by over one-third, and deliveries of imported plywood were down 19 per cent. Demand for woodpulp, used in the manufacture of paper products, was down nearly 40 per cent.

Deciduous woodland was the natural vegetation of Britain before the spread of agriculture and human settlement; as late as Roman times, more than one-third of the present-day UK was still covered in woodland; today only 9 per cent of the country has forest cover (in Europe, only Ireland has less). Although this is almost double the area in

1895, quality has not gone hand in hand with quantity. Since 1919, the Forestry Commission, a nationalized timber-producing agency, has been running an afforestation programme initially based on a belief that Britain would need wood in time of war. Although the strategic value of wood has long since declined, the Commission has continued to expand its activities regardless. It has planted conifers almost exclusively and now owns 42 per cent of UK woodland. Out of a total of 2.1 million hectares (5 million acres) of existing British woodland, half consists of conifer plantations planted within the past 40 years, using mainly introduced conifer species: Sitka spruce, Norway spruce, larch and lodgepole pine. Only 28 per cent of the plantations use our native Scots pine.

Much of this change has taken place at the expense of the UK's older woodlands – ancient woodlands and broadleaf forests of oak, beech and other native species, some over a century old, and ancient woodlands dating back centuries. About 405,000 hectares (nearly one million acres) of woodland were cleared during the two world wars, much of it established broadleaf woodland. The Nature Conservancy Council estimates that, since 1947, 30 to 50 per cent of Britain's ancient or semi-natural woodlands have been lost to agriculture or have been replaced by conifers. There are now about 250-300,000 hectares (600-740,000 acres) of ancient and semi-natural woodland left. Some is protected, much has been neglected as being of no commercial value, and some is maintained for hunting. Many of these woodlands are in small plots of ten hectares (25 acres) or less, making them particularly susceptible to agricultural intensification. In the trend towards bigger fields and more 'efficient' farming, many of these small woodlands are seen as obstacles and are in the process of being cleared.

Another, more recent, threat to forests comes from acid rain. Its effects in Europe are well known; less is known about how much it has affected British forests. The Forestry Commission has argued that acid rain is unlikely to pose a threat to our forests, but there is little hard evidence. Water authorities have also expressed increasing concern about the effects of acid rain. Surveys in 1978-80 revealed rainfall with an average pH of 4.2 to 4.7 in Scotland and northern England ('fresh' rain has a pH of 5.6); one preliminary survey found rain with a pH of 4.1 in southern England.[9] When acid levels in soil fall below pH 5, the soil's ability to support vegetation is affected. With consumption of coal and oil easing more slowly than it could, British forests could well be increasingly affected by acid rain.

Demand for wood and paper products not only encourages the replacement of ancient woodlands with conifer plantations, but has several knock-on effects through the services needed to support paper production. The paper and board industry is one of the biggest consumers of water in the country, using over one million tonnes of water per day for processing and cooling. Although the industry prides itself on its increased use of efficient water recycling, half the water used in processing – or about 170,000 tonnes per day – is nevertheless reduced to effluent containing cellulose and clay, and has to be discharged (after treatment) through sewers or into estuaries and coastal waters. The industry is also the sixth largest industrial consumer of energy. Although it generates one-third of its own electricity needs, this is half the amount it generated in 1965. The industry blames incoherent government energy policy which gives little support to industrial energy conservation. Paper also has to be transported, so the equivalent of 8,000 20-tonne trucks take to the roads every day to carry paper products.

British forests currently meet 5 per cent of the country's woodpulp needs. There are advantages in increasing this proportion, but not at the expense of Britain's natural woodland and wildlife. It makes far better sense to decrease demand and increase the proportion of recycled paper.

FISHERIES

To the east, north and west, the British Isles are surrounded by some of the richest fishing grounds in the world. Hence the important place fish takes in the British diet, and the long history and active record of the British fishing industry. So active has it been, in fact, that even the productive north-east Atlantic has not been able to keep up with demand from Britain and Europe, and over-fishing has long been a problem. As early as 1890, attempts to increase the yield of plaice were foiled by diminishing stocks. Since then, most of the staple species of the North Sea and north-east Atlantic have suffered.

Demand for herring grew to such a pitch that a complete ban on herring fishing in the North Sea was imposed in 1977. The EEC and Norway, which jointly own North Sea fish stocks, have now agreed the total annual catch of all North Sea species except herring. After lengthy negotiation within the EEC, the first full-scale herring fishery allowed in the North Sea for seven years was opened in May 1984. EEC fishing boats are now allowed an annual catch of 155,000 tonnes, of which the British share is 36,000 tonnes. But the absence of an agreement with Norway on herring stocks has led to fears that the same management problems that arose before the fishery was closed in 1977 will be repeated. Fisheries experts are also worried that Britain could have lost its taste for herring during the years when catches were banned.[10]

Fisheries are a renewable resource. If they are managed carefully, and catches are regulated, then they can in theory provide for most needs. If fish stocks are mismanaged and over-exploited, and are given insufficient time to breed and replenish themselves, the stocks will decrease, and the rates of replacement will decrease. The difficulty with controlling fish stocks is that most fish are found in international waters, and so are common property. Fishing often needs international regulation. The depletion of fisheries has led to repeated international disputes over fishing limits. Japan and the USSR have argued over the northern Pacific, and the US and several South American countries over the eastern Pacific tuna fishery.

Closer to home, the UK and Iceland fought a heated diplomatic battle in the 1970s over North Sea cod. Depletion of fish stocks led Iceland to extend its fishing limits four times between 1952 and 1975, bringing it up against British fishermen who had long used Icelandic waters as a major source of fish – nearly two-thirds of the UK's deep sea fish catch in 1976 came from these waters. As early as 1955, the UK embargoed Icelandic fish imports; by 1973 the dispute had escalated to the point where the interests of NATO were threatened: Iceland banned British military aircraft from its Keflavik air base, and Royal Navy frigates were sent to protect British trawlers. The low point of the dispute came in 1975, when Icelandic gunboats fired on British trawlers and cut their wires, and Iceland cut diplomatic ties with Britain.

The landed weight of British fish catches has been falling steadily. In 1977, just over 900,000 tonnes of fish were landed. By 1982, the total had fallen to just under 750,000 tonnes. The most frequently caught species in 1982 were mackerel (24 per cent of the total catch), haddock (17 per cent), cod (15 per cent), herring (6 per cent) and whiting (5 per cent). In May 1984, the government launched a three-year £7.9 million campaign to persuade people to eat more fish, arguing that consumption had fallen. In fact it is already on the rise. Although consumption of fish fell from 6.26 ounces per person per week in 1961 to a low of 4.17 ounces in 1977 (part of the reason being the supply problems that arose in the wake of shortages, notably of herring) consumption had, by 1982, climbed 20 per cent to 5.03 ounces.

It is not only open sea fisheries that are threatened. On Britain's coasts, stocks of mussels, cockles, shrimps and oysters face similar problems. Many of them depend on the ecosystems of estuaries, which are being steadily reclaimed for development and for landfill for domestic waste. Many major estuaries are near ports, where demand for space is growing, and breeding grounds are shrinking. There has been over-exploitation too. So many oysters have been taken from the Solent that public fishing rights have been curtailed. Coastal species are particularly susceptible to pollution from the discharge of sewage, industrial waste, used hot water from power stations, radioactive waste, and the spoil brought up by dredging.

TRANSPORT

Britain's road system is based on the era of the horse and cart. As hedgerows and fields are typical of British countryside, so winding streets and heavily congested roads are characteristic of British cities. A major opportunity for London was lost after the Great Fire of 1666, when Christopher Wren's plans to redesign the layout of the city along a more sensible grid pattern was rejected. British roads are barely designed to accommodate the motor vehicle at all, let alone in the numbers around today – there are nearly 20 million motorcycles, cars, vans and lorries on British roads, more than ever before.

The growth in the use of private cars is a critical issue. With the run-down of public transport during the 1960s, the development of motorways, and the emergence of the private car as a status symbol, the number of cars on the road rose dramatically during that period. It was predicted in the early 1960s that there would be 27 million vehicles on the road by 1980 and 40 million by 2010. Fortunately the present position is nowhere near so bad, but there are still nearly 16 million cars on British roads – two for every five adults compared to two for every six adults in 1971. The average Briton travels nine out of every ten kilometres in private cars.

It is absurd to see in Britain's larger cities in the early morning and early evening thousands of commuters, who daily drive from home to work and know all the pitfalls, sitting rigidly in traffic jams, breathing in noxious fumes, pushing their heart rates up with frustration, and stoically refusing to use public transport. Three out of five people travelling into central London by road every day travel by car – it takes 130,000 cars to carry them. If all Londoners travelling by road went by bus, it would take just 12,500 buses. The growth of the company car has added very considerably to the problems. Two out of every three miles travelled by British cars are clocked up by company cars, which are believed to account for between 42 per cent and 70 per cent of new car sales. Although in some cases these cars are an essential part of a person's job, in many cases they are not, being merely a luxury and status symbol.

New car sales in Britain are booming. A total of 1.79 million new cars were sold in 1983, a record year. Remarkably, the biggest growth area is in large-engined cars, and petrol consumption in the UK has increased by more than 20 per cent since 1972, despite the advent of more fuel-efficient cars. One of the reasons for this increase is that fuel has, in real terms, remained relatively cheap. Its real price was the same in 1978 as in 1973. Subsequently, it rose slightly before beginning to fall again in 1981. If world oil prices continue falling, consumption figures will rise even further. At the same time, the use of public transport has been on the decline. The number of journeys made by train has fallen by 17 per cent in the last ten years. The number of passenger journeys on London Transport alone has fallen by one-quarter. The implications are felt by everyone.

· Roads are congested, especially in cities and along major access routes. Traffic jams are the bane of city travel, and to find a parking space is a test of endurance. Towns and villages are assailed by heavy juggernauts.
· Road transport accounts for 20 per cent of Britain's total energy consumption, and nearly 60 per cent of its consumption of refined oil products. The average car uses nearly 1,360 litres (300 gallons) of petrol every year.
· Road transport generates eight million tonnes of carbon monoxide annually (90 per cent of airborne carbon monoxide), 500,000 tonnes of nitrogen oxides, 400,000 tonnes of hydrocarbons, and 7,400 tonnes of lead.[11]

- In 1981, nearly £40 million was spent on inland transport, or £700 for every person in the country. The average household spends 15 per cent of its income on transport.
- Britain's public transport has fallen far behind many other countries, often caught in a vicious cycle of high fares and few passengers. If too few people use it, the fares go up; if fares go up, fewer people use it. One estimate quoted by the *UK Response to the World Conservation Strategy* is that for every new car that takes to the road, 300 bus trips per year are lost.[12] In many other countries, the use of public transport is growing: systems are subsidized, fares are lower, services more dependable and efficient, and routes and networks are more extensive. In the last 20 years, the length of railway track in the UK has fallen from 17,000 miles to 11,000 miles, and the number of railway stations from 4,200 to 2,400. Between 1971 and 1981, the National Bus Company cut its mileage by one-quarter.[13]
- In 1982, nearly 6,000 people were killed and nearly 330,000 injured in road accidents. More than 98 per cent of those killed or seriously injured in road vehicle accidents were using private transport.
- The number of vehicles on the road has caused monumental headaches for traffic planners. London, one of the biggest cities in the world, has no effective central ring road and is only now gradually building an orbital by-pass. The North and South Circular is in some places a three-lane highway; in other parts a narrow one-lane suburban street. Plans to widen it in one particular spot – Ealing and Chiswick – have included proposals to cut down a magnificent row of horse chestnuts on Ealing Common, or to build a flyover that would cut West Chiswick in two. The problems are bad, the solutions worse. Only a reduction in road traffic will ease the pressure.
- More roads have had to be built. An average of 1,800 km of new roads are built every year. Assuming an average road width of six metres (motorways and dual carriageways are much wider), about 1,080 sq kms of land are being paved over every year by roads alone.

Government-imposed controls, such as higher road taxes or the introduction of tolls, would most likely be strongly opposed in Britain, although they have been used to good effect in other democracies. Much higher subsidies for public transport (and improved management) would be a more acceptable contribution. But in fact, much of the onus for change lies with the individual citizen, whose demand for goods causes much of the movement of commercial haulage traffic on the roads, and whose preference for mechanized mobility is behind the largest sector of road traffic: the private car.

POLLUTION

Thanks to its visibility, immediacy, and proven health risks, much has been done in the UK to control certain types of pollution. The Department of the Environment takes pleasure in pointing out there are once again salmon in the Thames, or that London now gets more winter sunshine than ever before because its skies are cleaner. But the battle is still far from won, and it cannot be won simply by relying on local or national authorities to act. Government spending on pollution control is falling. Not only is there evidence to suggest that many of the achievements of recent years may be undone as enforcement of controls is eased, but old problems persist and new problems are emerging, many of them consumer-linked:

· As the amount of traffic on the roads increases, so does atmospheric pollution in cities and towns. Traffic is the source of 28 per cent of the nitrogen oxide in the air over Britain. It also generates carbon, hydrocarbons, and heavy metals such as lead, which is added to petrol to improve engine performance. Links have been made between lead and permanent brain damage in children. Despite the success of the recent campaign against lead in petrol, the government is delaying the introduction of lead-free petrol on the grounds that EEC regulations will not come into effect until 1991. Technically, there is little to prevent lead-free petrol being introduced tomorrow.

· The straw burning that annually follows the harvest can cause uncontrolled fires, drifting smoke pollution that can impair health, and a reduction of visibility on roads that has already led to fatalities. Complaints about the practice have reached such a pitch that the National Farmers Union has been moved to warn its members to be more careful or else invite a total ban. The 1984 Royal Commission on Environmental Pollution recommended a total ban within five years.

· Soils, crops and rivers are being contaminated by chemical fertilizers and pesticides. One of the most toxic pesticides is 2,4,5-T, which is thought to be linked with cancers and birth defects and is banned in the United States; the US Environmental Protection Agency described 2,4,5-T as presenting 'unprecedented and overwhelming' risks to human health. It contains dioxin, which was responsible for

widespread contamination in 1976 when a chemical works blew up at
Seveso, near Milan. An explosion at a chemical factory in Derbyshire
in 1968 had similar consequences.
Yet it is still freely available in British garden centres. In June 1984,
the agricultural workers branch of the Transport and General
Workers Union issued a report criticizing the government's refusal to
ban its use, and listed 27 cases of death, cancer, birth deformities,
miscarriages and skin diseases among employees and their families
who had been in contact with 2,4,5-T.[14]

Fruit and vegetables can absorb chemicals from the air, the soil and
from fertilizers. Friends of the Earth has suggested that
advertisements for weedkillers and other pesticide sprays should carry
government health warnings, and that food labels should indicate the
amount of chemical residues left in them. A draft law has been
proposed by the Ministry of Agriculture that suggests giving
ministers powers to restrict the levels of residues in food meant for
human consumption.

· Rivers, lakes and coastal waters are being contaminated by the
discharge of untreated sewage and industrial waste. The Royal
Commission on Environmental Pollution warned in 1984 that many
bathing waters and beaches were contaminated to an undesirable
degree by sewage. Run-off of chemical fertilizers adds to the
problems: sewage and nitrogen fertilizers between them account for
most of the nitrates that enter drinking water. Nitrates can cause
methaemoglobinaemia, a condition in which the blood cannot carry
enough oxygen to meet the needs of the human body. In 1976, two
million people in East Anglia were supplied with drinking water with
more than the safe limit of nitrates recommended by the World
Health Organization.[15] During the 1984 drought, government
scientific advisers warned that any heavy rainfall between July and
October would wash more nitrogen fertilizers off the water-parched
land than usual, leading to serious nitrate pollution in rivers.

The release of untreated industrial waste into rivers and the sea has
contributed to the build-up of heavy metals such as mercury and
cadmium in water and fish. Heavy metals crop up regularly
elsewhere. Lead, for example, is found not only in emissions from
motor vehicles, but in domestic water pipes, paint and food.
Cadmium is used in several industrial processes and is also found in
phosphate fertilizers.

- Waste disposal is another problem. Research in 1984 revealed that cadmium, lead, mercury and other metals had been found in a field near a chemical waste processing plant at Bonnybridge in Scotland. Local inhabitants had become worried that there was a link between the plant and the incidence of cancer, deformed babies, diseased cattle and malformed or stillborn calves in the area. Fifty cows had died in the field where the tests were carried out.[16] The plant was closed in mid-1984.
- The production and disposal of toxic wastes, notably radioactive waste from nuclear power stations, is a continuing threat. No one knows precisely how much toxic waste is produced in Britain, and there is no government policy on toxic waste management. For instance, the Sellafield nuclear power station in Cumbria has been presenting problems since the 1950s. Sellafield discharges strontium, caesium and plutonium into the Irish Sea. While the plutonium accumulates on the sea bed near Sellafield, the strontium and caesium are carried by sea currents around the coast of Scotland into the North Sea fishing grounds and up the coast of Norway. In 1983, Greenpeace scored a major publicity coup by drawing attention to the discharge of nuclear waste from the plant into the Irish Sea. Sellafield had been shut down for annual maintenance work, and waste that should have been transferred to on-site storage tanks was discharged into the sea, contaminating a 30-mile stretch of beach. Greenpeace was fined £50,000, but the beaches were closed, public attention was drawn again to the dangers of radioactive discharge, and British Nuclear Fuels was prosecuted for allowing the leak and failing to keep discharges as low as possible.

    During 1984, Sellafield once again became the focus of the anti-nuclear power movement, whose disquiet regarding activities in the region seemed to be vindicated in July 1984 by the publication of a government report that pointed out that the level of leukaemia in the vicinity of Sellafield was one of the highest in Britain. There was no proof that the levels were connected with Sellafield, but the report nevertheless questioned the adequacy of controls over discharges from the plant.[17]

Pollution makes good newspaper copy and television time, and there are constant reminders of its dangers. New incidents usually produce TV news interviews with hapless representatives of the nuclear power industry or other polluting industry, whose normal defence is to point out the degree of speculation involved; 'there is no proof of the link' is a popular defence.

But while national energy or industrial policy have a great deal to answer for, they are ultimately determined largely by demand. It is easy to feel outraged at the effects of pollution and to castigate the industries responsible. But next time you are watching the latest nuclear power horror story unfold on TV, bear in mind that your TV is using electricity – and that a great deal of the business that comes the way of nuclear power stations is by courtesy your set and all the other sets in the country; and all the central heating systems, hi-fis, washing machines, dishwashers, ovens, immersion heaters, food processors, coffee percolators and other gadgets which demand electric power.

Every time a car is started, a heater switched on, or a lavatory flushed, pollution becomes just that much worse. To an extent this is unavoidable because of the system we are locked into. With the way much of today's energy is produced, for instance, we must use its pollutive services or go without. But consumers can control the extent to which they do the things that pollute. Less consumption of food, energy, services and goods, less use of private transport, and less waste of resources can all mean less pollution.

ENERGY

Energy is one of the major victims of the wasteful society. Its ready availability encourages the temptation to use far more than is necessary – cost is the only constraint that most people face at the moment. Even this gives British consumers little incentive, because prices are still fairly low in relative terms. In fact, there are two far more vital but less appreciated constraints: the limited stocks of fossil fuels we use most (coal, oil and gas supply 82 per cent of our energy), and the environmental impact of the way they are used.

The UK is heavily dependent on oil, coal and natural gas, and like many other industrialized countries will face upheaval over the next 20 to 30 years as these fuels become more scarce and expensive. Our own oil industry is no insurance against scarcity. Unless substantial new reserves are found, North Sea oil stocks are likely to begin tailing off in the 1990s. By then, the UK will be back to dependence on imported oil, with all the political and economic problems this will entail. The trend to new sources of energy – solar, wind and wave power for example – is slow, and mainly still in experimental stages. Besides which, the convenience of continuing to use oil, and the power of vested interests, will ensure that we will continue to rely overwhelmingly on fossil fuels for some time yet. Britain has managed to cut energy consumption by 10 per cent since 1973, but this has been due partly to falling industrial output, and partly to cuts in oil consumption forced on us by oil price rises. The amount of energy wasted is truly staggering. As teacher would say, there is room for improvement. The different elements in the supply chain illustrate the problems.

Primary energy is the total national supply of energy from all sources. The UK derives 37 per cent of its energy from oil, 35 per cent from coal, 23 per cent from natural gas, 4 per cent from nuclear power, and 1 per cent from hydro.

Delivered energy is the energy that actually reaches consumers, and amounts to much less than the energy generated, because 30 per cent of primary energy is lost during production, conversion and distribution. UK consumers use oil for 42 per cent of their energy needs, gas for 31 per cent, electricity for 14 per cent, and coal for 9 per cent. Industry is the biggest consumer, but is only just ahead of the domestic sector. In 1973, industry accounted for 43 per cent of delivered energy, but declining economic performance and energy use during the 1970s brought its share down to just under 32 per cent in 1982. In the same period, the share for private homes rose from 25 per cent to 29 per cent, and for transport from 16 per cent to 25 per cent. Total energy consumption peaked in 1979, since when it has fallen by nearly 12 per cent.

End use energy refers to how energy is actually used. In the UK, 66 per cent is used to heat buildings and to power industry, 26 per cent is used in transport, and 8 per cent is used in running lighting and electrical appliances.

Figure 1 shows that more than half the primary energy supplied in the UK is wasted, beginning with the losses sustained during its conversion and distribution and ending with inefficient use in the home or factory. Nearly 40 per cent of the energy supplied to British homes and 80 per cent of the energy supplied to transport is wasted. Most homes and road vehicles were designed and built when energy was relatively cheap and plentiful, and little was done to ensure that it was used efficiently.

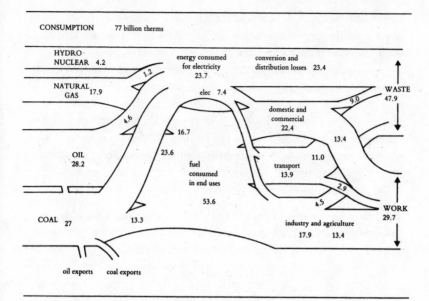

Figure 1: *Energy flow in the UK*

How is so much energy lost? Take buildings for example. Just over half the UK's primary energy is used to heat buildings, but they are so badly insulated that the bulk of the energy delivered is lost almost immediately. In a typical uninsulated semi-detached house, 35 per cent of heat losses go through the walls, 25 per cent through the roof, 15 per cent through the floor, 15 per cent through ventilation, and 10 per cent through windows. In most British houses, the ventilation rate is so high that all the air is completely replaced every 30 minutes.

Energy is also lost through inefficient heating systems. An open coal fire may look warm and inviting, but it is hopelessly inefficient: only between 5 and 30 per cent efficient. Most gas and coal boilers are 70 to 80 per cent efficient. Additionally, power stations themselves have poor thermal efficiency. Two-thirds of the heat generated by a power station is lost because of the low efficiency of converting coal to electricity – up to one-fifth of the UK's primary energy is lost through the cooling towers of power stations. So while an electric heater may be 100 per cent efficient in a front lounge, it is only 30 per cent efficient if losses at the power station and the national grid are taken into consideration.

The individual consumer accounts directly for all domestic demand for energy and much of the demand for transport – adding up to well over half the total energy used in this country. Add to this the amount of energy used in industry to meet consumer demands for goods and services, and domestic use ultimately accounts for well over two-thirds of British energy output – and a proportionate amount of energy wastage. Conservation and more efficient use would contribute enormously to savings in energy production and consumption. According to *A Low Energy Strategy for the UK*, if existing energy efficiency techniques were applied throughout the country, we would cut energy consumption by more than half – at no cost to our standard of living or level of economic activity.[18]

More than 82 per cent of British electricity is generated by coal-fired power stations. Electricity eats up 80 million tonnes of coal every year – more than 62 per cent of the UK's total coal production. The major users of electricity are private homes (39 per cent) and industry (36.7 per cent). Demand from both has fallen in the past ten years, but demand from shops and offices has increased by nearly half. And, although overall consumption has fallen off since the peak demand year of 1979, it is still higher than it was in 1972. One major side-effect of using coal is to increase the amount of sulphur dioxide in the atmosphere and so possibly to generate acid rain.

Demand for electricity is also behind one of the most controversial of all environmental issues – nuclear power. At the time of the 1973-74 oil crisis, nuclear power was widely hailed as the energy source of the future. The UK, Canada, France, West Germany and the US led in this field, and there were forecasts of more than 100 nuclear plants being built annually throughout the world. In the event, the nuclear power industry has not grown so dramatically. In 1983, there were 282 commercial reactors in 25 countries. Nuclear power currently provides about 14 per cent of Britain's electricity. If government building plans meet their targets, by the end of the century nuclear power will still generate only about one-fifth of total electricity supply in the UK, and so will not contribute much to easing dependence on oil and gas.

The negative aspects of nuclear power – problems with safety, waste disposal, and nuclear weapons proliferation – are well known, but astonishingly have not been enough to convince governments of the need to reassess its use. In the long run, the most telling factor may be that nuclear power is no longer economically attractive. In the US, nuclear power costs 65 per cent more than coal-fired power, and 25 per cent more than oil-fired power.[19] Despite this, the UK is pressing ahead with its nuclear programme, most notably with its plans to build a new reactor at Sizewell in Suffolk. This will be a pressurized water reactor of the kind that failed at Three Mile Island, and most of the opposition to the scheme has centred on the issue of safety. A public inquiry into the scheme was opened in 1983, but with the legal and technical support amassed by the CEGB at an estimated cost of £10 million, the hearing, at the time of this book going to press, appears to be rapidly becoming a formality. The CEGB spent £250 million on planning Sizewell even before the inquiry began, and is unlikely to write off so large an investment that easily.

[handwritten margin note: To expensive to sack]

One pointer for the future of electricity generation may be the Dinorwig power station in North Wales, opened in May 1984. Europe's biggest hydro-electric pumped storage power station, Dinorwig is built deep inside a mountain in Snowdonia. Water from an upper reservoir is channelled down tunnels to a lower reservoir. On the way it drops 1,800 feet down a surge shaft, turning six turbine generators which produce enough electricity to more than meet the entire demand for Wales. Cheap-rate electricity is then used to convert the turbines into pumps that take the water back to the upper reservoir. When plans for the station were first announced by the CEGB, conservationists expressed fears for the environmental effects on one of the most spectacular landscapes in Wales. In the event, the only sign of the station on the surface is a slate-dressed tunnel entrance. The station is non-pollutive, consumes no natural resources, and is invisible.

[handwritten margin note: less demand for nuclear]

In the end, the factor most likely to undermine the British nuclear programme is going to be decreased consumer demand. The CEGB predicts that electricity demand in the UK will grow at 1 per cent annually until at least 1990, and uses this as an argument to support its expansion plans. In fact, demand for electricity has been falling. It peaked in 1979, since when it has fallen by 8 per cent. A continued fall must ultimately discredit CEGB planning forecasts. These forecasts should also be amended to take into account the government's own, albeit limited, support for energy conservation. Conservation and greater use efficiency would not only reduce the demand for energy, but would reduce the consumption of oil, gas and coal, and reduce the negative environmental impacts of using fossil fuels. Energy conservation – using energy more efficiently and effectively – is now widely regarded as an alternative energy 'source' in its own right. Although the British government is encouraging energy conservation, investment in this country is between one-quarter and one-tenth the level in other EEC states.

The technology and advice to conserve energy has long been available to domestic British consumers, but the response has been mixed. Conservation in the home is on the increase, but so is consumption of petrol. Against the background of government investment in nuclear power and relatively paltry encouragement for conservation, reduced consumer demand offers far better hopes for reduced national demand for energy.

WATER

Water is one resource that is literally on tap and costs almost nothing to use. The average household water bill in 1983-84 was £6 per month. In a country where rain is a national joke, it seems absurd to suggest that water needs conserving. But simply being a well-watered country is not the end of the story. First, very little water is suitable for drinking until it has been treated, so treatment plants, reservoirs and pipelines have to be built. Second, water supply is uneven and there is no national water grid to spread the distribution. Third, something has to be done with waste water, which can contain chemicals and detergents. The ready and cheap availability of water encourages free use. Britain daily uses about 18.6 billion litres (4.1 billion gallons) of water. The biggest user is industry, followed by domestic use and agriculture. If direct domestic use is considered on its own, British consumers use about 125 litres (28 gallons) of water per person per day. But if the water used by industry and agriculture as part of the production process is included, then consumer demand – direct and indirect – accounts for the use of 330 litres (73 gallons) of water per person per day.

Until a decade ago, water supply was dictated by demand. If demand rose, new reservoirs would be built almost regardless of cost. Between 1960 and 1980, demand for water increased by more than one-third. But there is a limit both to the amount of space available for new schemes and to the resources of local water authorities. The result has been increasing emphasis on conservation. The inquiry into a scheme for a new reservoir at Broad Oak in Kent in 1979 was one of the first to hear long-range demand forecasts questioned, and the plans were finally rejected because it was agreed that the demand could be met with a less ambitious scheme. The inquiry also heard that between 20 per cent and 30 per cent of the water supplied to Kent consumers never reached them, because it leaked out through faulty mains.

The droughts of 1975-76 and 1984 showed people how consumption could be cut without having to resort to major sacrifices. In fact, during the drought of 1984, there was enough water overall in the country to meet demand. However, the drought also exposed the shortcomings of our water supply system, particularly the lack of a national water grid. Inequitable distribution meant some areas went without while others had a surplus. This meant an absurd situation of water shortages in the South West and such huge surpluses in Cumbria that water was being exported by tanker to Gibraltar – while North Devon still had water restrictions in October of that year. Asked at the height of the drought about plans for a national water grid, the minister in charge of drought action said that the capital expenditure needed could not be justified. The abundance of water in Cumbria is a classic example of supply overkill. Water engineers predicted that water demand in the area would grow, so the 1,086 hectare (2,680 acre) Kielder reservoir was built at a cost of £170 million. Since it opened in 1981, water demand in the area has been falling.[20]

During the 1984 drought, the Director-General of the Federation of Civil Engineering Contractors pointed out that the shortages caused by lack of rainfall were being aggravated by the fact that over one-quarter of the water pumped into British mains was lost through leaks.[21] In some areas, wastage through leaks is as high as 50 per cent.

Less than one-third of water supplies are metered. Where metering has been used in industry it has proved to be an effective incentive to conserve water.

WILDLIFE AND NATURE

The environmental problems raised by agriculture, forestry, transport, urban spread, pollution and the over-consumption of food, energy and other resources all have at least one thing in common – their effect on wildlife. British wildlife has long had to fit itself around people. The little we have now is all that remains after centuries of human ascendancy over nature. Today there are 1,423 flowering plant species, about 420 native mammal, bird, reptile, amphibian and fish species, and about 50,000 insects and other invertebrates. Nearly one-fifth of the plants in Britain alone are threatened. A 1970 survey by the Institute of Terrestrial Ecology estimated that the distribution of rare British flowering plants and ferns had fallen by 30 per cent between 1930 and 1960, and the number of very rare species had doubled since 1900.[22] Agriculture is implicated in the threats posed to half the rarest British animal and plant species. There is virtually no true wilderness left in Britain, and nowhere that wildlife is not affected in one way or another by human activity.

Until the Second World War, wildlife was relatively secure. Hedgerows and woodlands formed island habitats in seas of human activity; there was a reasonable amount of largely undisturbed moorland, wetland and upland available; and pollution – although a problem – was not as omnipresent as it has since become. The intensification of agriculture, however, and the increased burning of fossil fuels have meant that wildlife is no longer secure. The greatest threat to British wildlife is habitat loss.

· Hedgerows have been removed to make bigger fields that are easier to plough; between 1946 and 1972 they were being taken out at a rate of 7,250 km (4,500 miles) per year.[23] By 1972, about 80 per cent of the hedgerow trees present in 1945 had also been removed.[24] Hedgerows have traditionally been an important wildlife sanctuary, being the site of about 280 plant species alone. The *Conservation and Development Programme for the UK* quotes one estimate that further hedgerow removal could seriously affect 70 to 80 species.[25]
· Woodland has been cleared; some of our ancient woods date back thousands of years, and have played a vital role in rural life and as habitats for wildlife. Between 1945 and 1975, clearance for agriculture and conversion to conifer plantations for commercial forestry destroyed nearly one-third of Britain's ancient woodlands.[26]
· The farming revolution has caused a marked rise in the use of chemical pesticides and inorganic fertilizers; the use of nitrogen-based fertilizers alone increased eight-fold between 1953 and 1976,[27] and there are now over 800 kinds of pesticide on the market. Despite all the warnings about the dangers of using DDT (which, among other things, reduces fertility in birds of prey and nearly made the peregrine falcon extinct in the UK), it is still in use.

· Heathland is being lost. There are claims, for instance, that Dorset will have lost all its heaths by 1990. The area has already been reduced by half since 1962, whittling away the habitat of rare species such as the sand lizard, the smooth snake and the Dartford warbler.
· About 100,000 hectares (250,000 acres) of wetland are drained annually,[28] threatening all the birds, plants and fish that rely on wetland ecosystems. A plan announced in August 1984 (and fortunately dropped the following month) to drain Otmoor – a low-lying marshy area near Oxford – for farmland could have led to a 45-cm drop in the level of the Cherwell and destroyed natural habitat supporting kingfishers, herons, snipe and redshank, and flora such as spotted orchids, cowslips, marsh marigolds, and snake's head fritillaries. The benefits? An increase in milk production of nearly half a million litres per year (at a time when EEC milk surpluses are already embarrassing), of cereal production by 2,170 tonnes per year, and of farmers' income by £350,000 per year.[29]
· Less than 15 per cent of the lowland bogs once found in northern England and Scotland now remain. Downland and moorland has also been ploughed up; one-fifth of Exmoor's moorland alone was lost between 1947 and 1976;[30] and one-fifth of our chalk grassland was converted to agriculture between 1966 and 1980.

Over 40 per cent of Britain's countryside is designated as protected land, ranging from national parks to green belts and nature reserves (see Figure 2). On paper that sounds impressive. In practice, protection is minimal. Three examples illustrate some of the problems.

· There are ten national parks in England and Wales. (Scotland, with some of the finest landscape and habitat in the British Isles, has none.) They make up about 9 per cent of the land area, mostly in the uplands. Unlike national parks in many other countries, they are not fully protected but are still actively farmed and developed. They are also anything but 'national' – nearly three-quarters of national park land is still privately owned or managed. Just over 1 per cent is owned by national park authorities, and the rest is shared between the Forestry Commission (8 per cent), the National Trust (7.5 per cent), water authorities (3.9 per cent) and other public or semi-public bodies.[31] The Ministry of Defence owns or leases four times as much national park land as the national park authorities. Military firing ranges occupy 78 per cent of Dartmoor's northern moorland plateau,

AREAS	SQUARE KM
Total land area of UK	244,100
Green Belts and Areas of Great Landscape Value (non-statutory designation)	39,694
Areas of Outstanding Natural Beauty (England, Wales, Northern Ireland only)	17,085
Sites of Special Scientific Interest (England, Wales, Scotland only)	13,614
National parks (England, Wales only)	13,600
National Scenic Areas (Scotland only)	10,015
Areas of Scenic Interest (Northern Ireland only)	7,400
National Nature Reserves	1,366
Others (local and county trust nature reserves, RSPB and National Trust properties, country parks)	3,090
Total	105,864
Percentage of total land area	43.4%

Figure 2: *Major areas designated for conservation and recreation*

taking in some of the finest moors and valleys in the park.

· There are 32 Areas of Outstanding Natural Beauty (AONBs) in England and Wales, which make up 10 per cent of the total land area. Four more have been designated, and eight in Northern Ireland. Pye-Smith and Rose call them one of the most useless of countryside designations.[32] Administered by the Countryside Commission, they are not protected from development by farmers, foresters or industries, and there is prevailing confusion about what they are supposed to achieve. They certainly have no special status as areas for conservation or recreation, yet some AONBs – notably the Chilterns and the Dorset Downs – have many of the characteristics of national parks and are widely thought to merit a greater degree of conservation than at present.

· The Nature Conservancy Council (NCC) is responsible for Sites of Special Scientific Interest (SSSIs). Nearly 3,900 sites covering 5.6 per cent of the land area have been designated, but the NCC has no powers beyond persuasion to stop SSSIs being developed, reclaimed or 'improved'. Despite all the new SSSIs currently being designated by the NCC, Britain is currently losing about one site per day. In Kent alone, 40 per cent of SSSIs have been destroyed or damaged since 1951, and 60 per cent of SSSIs on the chalk downs of Wiltshire have suffered losses to agricultural improvement.

Not all changes in land use have resulted in the destruction of wildlife. There is already evidence that wildlife has moved into new ecological niches in and around human development; it has done this in the British Isles for centuries. Wild plants colonize derelict urban land; there are more foxes per square kilometre in Bristol than anywhere else in the world; where land is left vacant long enough, incipient woodland emerges. But the degree of change in the countryside has never been so rapid as it has been since the war. Wildlife a century ago might have been able to adapt to changes. Now it is being given fewer and fewer options, and its margin of survival is narrower than it has ever been.

BRITISH ENVIRONMENTAL ORGANIZATIONS

The welfare of the British environment is divided between the government and its related statutory bodies, and the voluntary movement. Government policy on the environment is largely weak, ineffectual and confused, and supportive of the very forces of production that initiate most of the problems, particularly agriculture and forestry. Most of the work is left – as it traditionally has been – to voluntary organizations.

The government sector

No one government department is responsible for environmental matters. The misleadingly named Department of the Environment (DoE) was a politically expedient union in 1970 of the former ministries of transport, public housing and works, and local government. Transport was hived off in 1976. The DoE claims to be responsible for a wide range of functions which affect people's living environment. In practice, this largely means the functioning of the urban environment. Environmental protection, the countryside, recreation, pollution and waste disposal all come under its brief, but in each area it has proved itself singularly uninspired and ineffective. The DoE severely limits its funding of the Nature Conservancy Council and the two Countryside Commissions, and influences their policy by appointing senior staff to these organizations. *DOE coopts the NCC & 2 CC's.*

At the London launch of the World Conservation Strategy in 1980, the then Secretary of State, Michael Heseltine, spoke grandly of 'a philosophical approach totally in line with a sensible conservation policy [and] . . . a personal commitment that starts from a simple premise: in any individual decision, the starting point must be to conserve what matters. Those who have a contrary objective must bear the onus of proof'. What has happened since – including the emasculation of the Wildlife and Countryside Act – has given little indication of any real DoE interest in 'conserving what matters'.

NCC not active enough

The Nature Conservancy Council (NCC) is the closest organization Britain has to a state conservation department, but is the subject of much criticism from conservationists for its failure to take a more active stance in defending natural areas against farming and forestry. It is responsible for managing 181 National Nature Reserves (NNRs), for commissioning research and making grants, and for 'advising' the government on nature conservation policies. Only one-third of NNRs are owned by the NCC – the rest have to be protected by management agreements taken out with the owners, who are often farmers. How long the NCC will be able to continue paying farmers the difference in lost production is unclear.

NCC gives subsidy to farmers for lost production

2

The Countryside Commission for England and Wales replaced the National Parks Commission in 1968, a year after the setting up of the Countryside Commission for Scotland. The two Commissions are responsible for providing grants for public access to the countryside, helping to designate country parks, Areas of Outstanding Natural Beauty (AONBs), and Heritage Coasts, and (in England and Wales) for 'formulating policy' for national parks. Neither Commission owns any land and, like the NCC, both are frequently criticized for the weakness of their defence of nature against farming and forestry. There is some confusion about what AONBs are intended to achieve; there is also confusion over the aims of the Commissions.

The Department of Energy is charged with the 'co-ordinated and effective development' of Britain's energy and with 'promoting economy and efficiency in the supply, distribution, use and consumption of fuel and power'. Its conservation division has promoted domestic, industrial and commercial energy efficiency and conservation with only limited success. The Department's energy conservation record certainly did not impress Peter Walker when he took over the department following the 1983 general election: 'I was staggered to find out what little progress had been made in this field', he observed. 'The production side of this department is a go-ahead concern but the energy efficiency side is awful'.[33] In 1983, the department spent £15 million on conservation, an increase of £4 million on 1982.

At the same time, the Department of Energy is responsible for the general policy of the nationalized energy industries – and thus for the lack of progress in curbing sulphur dioxide emissions from coal-fired power stations, for the lack of progress in making electricity generation more efficient, and for the continuing promotion of nuclear power.

The Ministry of Agriculture, Fisheries and Food (MAFF) is responsible for national policy on agriculture and fisheries. While it is responsible for food distribution and public health standards in the manufacture, preparation and distribution of basic foods, MAFF is also responsible for the continuing intensification of agriculture at the expense of the natural environment, for the system of farming subsidies (including the Common Agricultural Policy), and for existing levels of pesticide residues and additives in home-produced food. Agriculture is subject to almost no planning control, landowners being subject only to voluntary controls over how they use their land. Some landowners agree to the absurd system whereby they are paid by the NCC to keep their land out of production. MAFF has remained deaf to the constant appeals from conservationists for a reform of the present system and for more planning control.

The voluntary sector

In contrast to the prevailing inefficacy of government activity on environmental protection, the voluntary sector has initiated most of the pressure for change, has identified many of the basic problems, their causes and solutions, and, where the government has prevaricated, has itself stepped in to acquire land for conservation, influenced government decisions, and mobilized public support. And it has been doing so for more than a century.

123

British voluntary environmental pressure groups have a combined membership of about three million, making the environmental movement one of the largest mass movements in British history. The interests of pressure groups range from nuclear power to butterfly conservation.

The biggest landowning group is the National Trust, which is the biggest charity in the country, with a membership of 1.5 million and a 1983 income of £48 million (compare this to the NCC budget of £10 million). Land owned by the National Trust is inalienable, and the Trust has become one of the biggest landowners in the country; its 162,000 hectares (400,000 acres) include areas of considerable natural value. It owns, among other things, nearly one-quarter of the Lake District national park. Pye-Smith and Rose describe the Trust's relationship to conservation as 'analogous to the relationship of the Vatican to Christianity: it is always in the rearguard. The Trust studiously avoids the pressure group image, which it scarcely needs considering its immensely powerful connections within the corridors of power'.[34]

Other major conservation charities include the Royal Society for Nature Conservation (RSNC), which co-ordinates the country's 42 county nature trusts, which between them manage 145,000 hectares (360,000 acres) of nature reserves, the Royal Society for the Protection of Birds (RSPB), a combined landowner, fund-raiser and pressure group that is the largest conservation body in Europe and one of the most effective and professional in the UK, and the Council for the Protection of Rural England (CPRE), whose main interest is landscape conservation. Like the RSPB, it has considerable influence in political circles, and has been actively campaigning for a reassessment of agriculture and forestry priorities. CPRE has recently widened its brief to include transport and energy.

Although primarily known as an international conservation body, World Wildlife Fund UK spends much of its money on conservation in this country, for which it receives less credit than perhaps it should. Its policy of a professional approach to fund-raising is felt by some to have distanced the Fund from its fundamentally charitable principles, but it does nevertheless raise about £2.8 million annually for British conservation (although its administrative costs are high).

More overtly activist are campaigning groups such as Friends of the Earth (FoE) and Greenpeace. FoE was at the forefront of the environmental movement during its most active years at the beginning of the 1970s. It has recently emerged from a long spell of internal dissension, caused by problems between directors and staff and between headquarters and the 250 local supporters groups.[35] Its main interests are energy, transport, wildlife, the countryside and waste. Greenpeace is best known for its direct action tactics, designed to highlight commercial whaling and sealing, radioactive waste dumping and the testing of nuclear weapons.

REFERENCES

1 Rose, Chris (1984) Wildlife: The battle for the British countryside. In Wilson, D (ed) *The Environmental Crisis*. Heinemann, London

2 Shoard, Marion (1980) *The Theft of the Countryside*. Temple Smith, London

3 Baldock, David (1984) Land use: A test of priorities. In Wilson, D *op cit*

4 Mellanby, Kenneth (1975) *Can Britain Feed Itself?* Merlin Press, London

5 Green, Bryn (1981) *Countryside Conservation*. George Allen and Unwin, London

6 UKWCS (1983) *The Conservation and Development Programme for the UK: A Response to the World Conservation Strategy*. Kogan Page, London

7 *The Times* (1984) 27 July

8 UKWCS (1983) *op cit*

9 Royal Commission on Environmental Pollution (1984) *Tenth Report*. HMSO, London

10 *The Times* (1984) 29 May

11 Hamer, Mick (1984) Transport: Why we have to control the car. In Wilson, D *op cit*

12 UKWCS (1983) *op cit*

13 Hamer, Mick (1984) *op cit*

14 *The Times* (1984) 6 June

15 Price, Brian (1984) Pollution: "The invisible violence". In Wilson, D *op cit*

16 *The Times* (1984) 2 August

17 *The Times* (1984) 24 July

18 Leach, Gerald *et al* (1979) *A Low Energy Strategy for the United Kingdom*. IIED, London

19 Brown, Lester *et al* (1984) *State of the World 1984*. W W Norton, New York

20 Pye-Smith, Charlie and Rose, Chris (1984) *Crisis and Conservation*. Penguin, Harmondsworth

21 *The Times* (1984) 9 July

22 UKWCS (1983) *op cit*

23 Shoard, Marion (1980) *op cit*

24 Rose, C (1984) *op cit*

25 UKWCS (1983) *op cit*

26 Shoard, Marion (1980) *op cit*

27 Rose, C (1984) *op cit*

28 Ibid

29 *The Times* (1984) 20 August

30 Shoard, Marion (1980) *op cit*

31 MacEwan, A and M (1982) *National Parks: Conservation or Cosmetics*. George Allen and Unwin, London

32 Pye-Smith, C and Rose, C (1984) *op cit*

33 *The Times* (1983) 1 November

34 Pye-Smith, C and Rose, C (1984) *op cit*

35 Ibid

CONSERVATION BEGINS AT HOME

5

The root causes of the environmental crisis in the North are over-consumption and waste. We demand more than we need; we waste more than we should. Driven by the quest for affluence and status, and by the belief that consumption and material acquisition is the route to the good life, we demand food, shelter, clothing, energy, transport, medical services, recreation, commodities and other services. To provide all this, resources have to be tapped, processed, packaged, marketed and supplied. Land has to be farmed to provide food; houses have to be built to provide shelter; energy has to be generated to provide warmth; roads have to be built to provide transport; forests have to be cut to provide wood.

But exploitation in itself is not the problem. The earth has the potential capacity to support many more people than at present. Conservation does not mean stopping all consumption and all development. It is not so much a matter of *what* we use as of *how* we use it. Conservation means regulating consumption and development to ensure a steady, continuing, adequate and equally shared supply of resources and services.

If conservation is living within our means, then the North is guilty of living beyond its means. Take energy for example. A Briton consumes 100 times as much energy as a Bangladeshi and 36 times as much as a Kenyan. Americans consume more than twice as much energy as Britons; the average American consumes as much energy as 221 Bangladeshis.[1] Most of the energy Britons use is not actually 'used' but wasted because it is used inefficiently. We could substantially reduce our energy demands without any changes in our way of life. There would still be petrol in our cars, hot water in our taps, and warm rooms in our homes in winter.

It is a fallacy to believe that consumption and acquisition are preconditions for a good standard of living. A good life – if not a better life – can be achieved (and by far more people) with far less consumption. Consumerism makes little distinction between necessity and luxury. It also overlooks three basic principles:

1. Most natural resources are infinite in quantity, but only so long as we live off the interest and not the capital. There are infinite supplies of food, forests, fresh air, and water, but they will continue to be available only if they are managed and used rationally.
2. Everything is connected. Resource depletion and environmental destruction are not always isolated and limited, but have knock-on effects in both time and space.
3. Things do not disappear when we throw them away. They are never 'consumed' in the sense of being used up. They merely change form. One man's 'waste' is another man's environmental problem.

WASTE

Waste is a uniquely human characteristic. While most species and organisms use their environment economically, driven largely by their survival instinct, the complexity of the human psyche creates many more diverse impulses and needs which must be satisfied. For humans, once materials and resources have fulfilled an immediate need they are often regarded as useless. In fact, nothing is totally useless. Every material, except possibly plastics, can be used again, often indefinitely.

Humans have probably been wasteful since they first evolved from a primitive state, but the truly wasteful society of today emerged after the Second World War. People became used to having things on tap in the quantities they wanted. The concept of 'consumerism' was born. With so much available, people reckoned they could afford to dispose of the 'old' when the 'new' came on to the market. Waste and disposability became unconscious activities which were questioned almost as little as consumption. Waste has indeed become a part of consumption.

Why does waste matter?

· Waste consigns materials which could be used again to the rubbish tip. If the materials consumed were recycled, our demand for the raw stocks of the materials would diminish and we would reduce the pressure on the environment. Less demand for paper would mean less demand on forests. Less demand for food would mean less demand for agricultural land.

- The manufacture of glass, metal products, paper and other materials uses energy. Throwing away an aluminium beer can or a copy of *The Times* has been compared to pouring out the equivalent of a beer can half filled with petrol. Recycling these materials would reduce the energy needed in materials production by between 50 and 90 per cent.[2]
- The production of iron, steel and aluminium creates more pollution than their recycling. Recycling iron and steel scrap, for example, reduces the amount of airborne pollution given off by using coke in iron ore reduction.
- Unrecycled waste does not magically disappear. It has to be disposed of, and this means in rubbish tips or in landfill. Nearly 90 per cent of all Britain's municipal waste is buried in landfill. Many solid wastes cause serious pollution problems, notably when they are discharged into rivers and oceans.

There is a great deal of truth in the adage 'waste not, want not'. Reducing waste reduces demand for resources, which reduces the likelihood of future shortages. Waste can be reduced by using resources more efficiently, curbing over-consumption, and recycling materials that cannot be reused in their existing form. Despite the environmental and economic advantages of recycling, and the publicity given to it in the last 10 to 15 years, only about one-quarter of the world's paper, aluminium and steel is recovered and recycled, and most of this is done within the industry concerned rather than after the consumer has finished with it. Nevertheless, even this little has generated an international trade in recyclable materials, and has produced substantial savings in capital and energy. Citizen demand for better use of resources has been behind Japan's success in recycling, which has, for example, reduced Hiroshima's volume of refuse by 40 per cent.

There are no material or legal incentives for Britons to recycle materials. It is easy and convenient to throw waste into the rubbish bin, have the local council take it away, and just forget about it. Every week, the average British household wraps up nearly 15kg (33 lbs) of materials in a black plastic bag which the local council takes away and buries. Household garbage annually weighs in at about 43 million tonnes, of which less than 1 per cent is recycled, about 10 per cent burned and the rest buried in landfill. The contents of household waste vary according to the area, but of that 15kg (33 lbs), about 9kg (20 lbs) is paper, metal and glass that could be recycled, and about 2.5kg (6 lbs) is vegetable waste that could be put into compost heaps. Reclamation and recycling are unlikely to be undertaken on any significant scale by local or national governments in the forseeable future. But the householder can take action now. With very little effort, most households could cut their garbage output from 15kg to about 3kg or less.

There are two basic principles to reducing waste:

1. Before you buy or use something, ask yourself whether or not you really need it.
2. Before you throw something away, ask yourself whether or not it could be reused, recycled or passed on to someone else.

Paper

More than one-third of the world's annual commercial wood harvest is turned into paper. Only about one-quarter of that paper is currently recycled, but the technical means already exist to enable this figure to be doubled in the next 15 years. That would meet almost 75 per cent of new paper demand, equivalent to freeing eight million hectares of woodland (nearly four times the total UK woodland area) from paper production.[3] Britain currently recycles about one-third of its paper. This figure compares badly with the world's leaders in recycling – Mexico, Japan, the Netherlands and Spain – which recycle between 40 and 50 per cent of their paper, but compares well with most other European countries (22 to 35 per cent) and the United States (27 per cent). Japan (the world's second largest consumer of paper) and the Netherlands have been driven to recycling because they are crowded and land-poor; waste dumps are frowned upon as a waste of land. Municipal authorities have been forced to encourage recycling. Japan has encouraged people to sort their waste and take it along to local material collection centres. Waste exchanges in West Germany, the Netherlands and Sweden have helped to encourage trade in waste materials.

Britain annually uses more than seven million tonnes of paper and board – 125kg (275 lbs) per person. Although that is well down on the US figure of 301kg (663 lbs) per person, it is one of the highest figures in Europe and, like all Northern figures, is vastly more than the amount of paper used in the South. India for instance uses 2kg (4.5 lbs) of paper per person per year. About three-quarters of our paper, board and woodpulp (ground or 'cooked' wood used in paper-making) needs are imported. The other quarter comes from recycled paper.

Of the newsprint used in the UK, only about 12 per cent is home produced (down from 50 per cent in 1969). This is mainly because the cheapest newsprint comes from those countries with major forests where mills can turn wood into newsprint quickly and economically. Sweden, Finland and Norway supply 45 per cent of our needs. Britain uses 1.38 million tonnes of newsprint per year. That is about 170g (6 ozs) of paper per adult every day – the equivalent of one copy of *The Times* and the *Sun* for each adult per day.

Paper recycling has two major benefits. First, it takes pressure off the world's forests. Finland and Sweden between them are the source of nearly half Britain's paper and woodpulp imports, and another 25 per cent comes from Canada and the United States.[4] Home-produced woodpulp accounts for less than 1 per cent of British needs. Second, recycling waste paper could reduce household garbage by more than one-third, thereby reducing the amount of land buried under landfill. Burning waste paper has been tried in several countries, notably the United States, but waste paper used as a fuel is worth only about one-third to one-half of its value in recycling.

Although the British government officially encourages recycling within the paper and board industry, there are few public paper collection centres in Britain. This leaves the consumer with four choices.

· Contact your local council and find out if they have any paper recycling schemes. If they do not have one, try to persuade them to start one. Sound out local feeling, and establish the degree of demand for such a scheme. Speak to your MP.
· Start your own paper collection scheme, and either get council support or operate it in aid of a local charity, which may offer to provide publicity and voluntary help. This will mean establishing a collection system, making sure it is well publicized, arranging collection points, and negotiating prices and collection with a waste paper merchant. The British Waste Paper Association gives advice.
· Arrange a paper recycling scheme at work. Encourage people to store their waste paper in separate bins, and have it periodically collected by a paper recycling company.
· Save your paper in a spare cupboard or outside store and periodically take it along to a local waste paper merchant.

Aluminium
Demand for aluminium as a lighter substitute for steel has grown

considerably in recent decades. It is used for everything from beverage cans to household appliances and jet aircraft. Some analysts believe that up to 80 per cent of all aluminium could be recycled, but in 1981 the figure for recycled aluminium was closer to 30 per cent.[5] This has meant more bauxite mining and greater demand for the coal needed in extracting aluminium from the bauxite. Producing raw aluminium uses up 20 times as much electricity as does recycling the metal. As energy costs rise, so the case for increasing the amount of aluminium recycled gains ground.

Each Briton directly uses about 9kg (20 lbs) of aluminium every year, the equivalent of over 1,000 soft drink cans. The amount of aluminium recycled in Britain has fallen from a high of 36 per cent in 1965 (more than anyone but West Germany) to 28 per cent today – below the world average. The world leaders in recycling are the Netherlands (42 per cent) and Italy (41 per cent). Italy produces half its aluminium needs from scrap.

Alcoa of Great Britain launched a Cash-a-Can scheme in 1979, with plans to have 20 regional collection centres in the country by 1985, paying 25p per kilo for aluminium scrap. But results were disappointing. Only 14 million cans were recycled in 1982, falling very short of the target of 33 million. A centre at King's Cross in London was closed down within months because of poor response. Alcoa eventually closed the scheme down because it was no longer making cans in the UK, leaving the country without a comprehensive national aluminium recycling scheme. Some local authorities and community groups (particularly in London) still run recycling schemes though.

· Find out from your local council or nearest scrap merchant if there is a local recycling scheme. If there is not, you could either arrange to deliver your scrap aluminium (along with other metals) to the nearest scrap merchant, or even consider starting a recycling scheme. Community groups often launch schemes to raise money, advertising locally for people to bring in scrap and selling it to scrap merchants.

Glass

Britain annually uses 5,900 million glass containers, or 105 bottles and jars per person. Producing all the glass to make the containers uses up nearly two million tonnes of raw materials and a considerable amount of energy. Yet the average Briton throws away 97 of those 105 containers, which are carted away by refuse collectors and buried out of sight, never to be used again. That amounts to about £350 million worth of materials (all of which could be reused) and millions of pounds worth of energy.

Glass is made from sand, limestone, soda-ash and cullet (waste glass). The proportion of cullet was, until 30 to 40 years ago, about 20 per cent, but improved technology has allowed manufacturers to increase the proportion without sacrificing the quality of glass. The proportion of cullet could eventually be as high as 50 per cent; the Swiss have already achieved 60 per cent in some of their glass.[6] Glass has been recycled as long as cullet has been used, but it has only been in the last ten years that Europe has had a concerted public recycling programme. Twelve countries are now involved, and the amount of glass recycled has doubled since 1980. Britain launched its Bottle Bank scheme in 1977. In that first year, five district councils took part and 261 tonnes of glass were recovered. By 1983, there were 1,750 bottle banks in 286 council areas, and nearly 72,000 tonnes were being recovered. The scheme has become the most effectively organized recycling programme in the country. But Britain still lags behind the rest of Europe. While we recycle a modest 8 per cent of our glass (less than anyone else in Europe), the Dutch recycle almost half, the Swiss 42 per cent, the Belgians almost one-third, the West Germans 30 per cent, and the French 24 per cent.

London's efforts are particularly modest. London households annually generate 3.25 million tonnes of garbage, of which 300,000 tonnes is glass – about one-sixth of all the glass containers used every year in Britain. Even if only one-third of this figure was to be recycled, it would put Britain well up the European league. But Londoners have responded to the call by recycling only 8,500 tonnes of glass – about 3 per cent of their annual consumption.

The benefits of recycling are many. The more glass that is recycled, the less sand, limestone and soda-ash that has to be quarried. Some of Britain's best limestone is quarried in environmentally sensitive areas such as the Peak District and the Yorkshire Dales. Recycling reduces the volume of garbage that has to be disposed of. If Londoners were to recycle all their glass containers, the amount of garbage produced by the city would drop by nearly 10 per cent. Recycling means less energy is used in glass production. The amount of glass currently recycled in Britain saves the equivalent of 100,000 barrels of oil per year. If we were to recycle just half our glass, we would save the equivalent of 715,000 barrels.

Environmentalists are divided about the relative merits of recycling glass and encouraging beverage manufacturers to use returnable bottles. To reuse a bottle many times over – many people already do it every day with milk bottles – would save even more energy than recycling scrap glass. It has been estimated that although a returnable bottle scheme in the United States would cost 40,000 existing jobs, it would nevertheless create 165,000 new jobs.[7] Friends of the Earth has been campaigning for a returnable bottle programme in Britain since its first publicity stunt: dumping 1,500 bottles on the doorstep of Schweppes headquarters in 1971. A returnable deposit on bottles would probably encourage more people to take part in glass reuse. But until manufacturers and the government agree to the idea, recycling through Bottle Banks remains the only available option.

The Glass Manufacturers' Federation estimates that about one person in ten uses a bottle bank, although in some areas the proportion is as high as one in four. The rate usually depends on the commitment of the local authority. Hence, while the national average is 2.8kg (6 lbs) of glass recycled per person, the borough of Reading and Bracknell recycles 10kg (22 lbs) per head. One hurdle to cross is convincing local authorities to take part in the Bottle Bank scheme. With budgets being cut back, many are reluctant to dig into their pockets to pay for the skips and for the storage and transport costs involved. But most schemes pay for themselves, and may even bring in small profits. The biggest obstacle is persuading people to take part.

· Support your local bottle bank. If there is no bottle bank, write to your local authority, MP or newspaper. Ask them whether there are any plans to introduce one in your area. Keep pressing, until the local authority either sets one up or gives a watertight reason why it cannot.

Iron and steel

Theoretically, using electric arc furnaces, it should be possible to recycle nearly all the iron and steel we use. This would cut energy costs by 75 per cent and capital requirements by half, and make steel production cheaper. About 45 per cent of the world's steel is currently recycled, with some countries using scrap for 60 to 75 per cent of the metal used in steel making. But only one-quarter of this is scrap reclaimed after use by consumers, and the proportion is falling.[8]

The UK is one of the smallest consumers of steel and one of the most active recyclers. We use about 325kg (715 lbs) of steel per person per year (half the figure of Japan, and 60 per cent that of West Germany), and recover about 35 per cent of our scrap (second only to Belgium at 40 per cent). But less than 10 per cent of recycled scrap comes from consumers – the majority is recycled within the industry.

- Reduce your demand for metal products and implements by making them last longer.
- Save your scrap metal and periodically take it to the nearest scrap metal merchant. Check your local Yellow Pages for addresses.

Packaging

Packaging makes up about one-third of all household waste. Some packaging is necessary for health, safety and protection of the contents, but most packaging is simply aesthetic, designed to be used once (and briefly) and then thrown away. It is part of the marketing process of a free enterprise society. Not only does packaging account for a large part of the cost of some products (for example, aerosol cans, perfume bottles and tinned foods), but costs increase when the packaging is simply thrown away. About 42 per cent of all paper used in Britain is used for wrapping and packaging.

- Reduce your use of all packaging. Decline the offer of paper bags to carry goods home unless you really need them. Do not be fooled by extravagant packaging that diverts attention from the quality of the product.

Plastics

Plastics have replaced many of the manufacturing materials once commonly used, and present two problems: they cannot normally be recycled, and because they are not biodegradable (capable of being decomposed by living matter) they do not break down when they are buried in rubbish dumps. The only way to reduce the amount of plastic thrown out with the garbage is to reduce the amount of plastic passing through the home. Buy soft drinks in glass bottles that can be recycled rather than in plastic bottles that need to be thrown away. Reuse plastic shopping bags.

In 1982, Imperial Chemical Industries began running trials in Leeds and Bradford with plastic bottle banks. The company is hoping to encourage people to recycle larger soft drink and beer bottles made from polyethylene terephthalate (pet). ICI is doubling its capacity to make pet-type plastic bottles.

Consumer durables

Consumer durables present a real resource problem. Many manufactured goods are not designed to last. They either wear out, go out of fashion, or are superseded by improved models. Obsolescence is built in. Status compels many people to settle for nothing less than present generation products, yet there is rarely any rational reason why new should replace old if the old performs the intended task. If a 30-year-old vacuum cleaner (built to last) still cleans the house, why replace it with a new (and often less durable) model? Why buy a new electric typewriter when the old manual does the job required?

True, manufacturers make it difficult to keep using old equipment. A 20-year-old stove may work perfectly well, but may have to be discarded for want of a spare part no longer available. However, a few basic precautions can lessen some of the ill-effects of the throwaway society.

· Buy well, and support craftsmanship. It pays off in the long run. Buying goods on the cheap is false economy. A cheap radio may cost one-third as much as an expensive radio, but it probably lasts only one-third of the time, or less. If you buy cheap, you often end up paying just as much in repair bills or completely replacing a worn out model. In the process, more resources are consigned to the waste heap.
· Do not be put off by the insistence of a manufacturer that a broken object is irrepairable; ask someone who runs a small local repair shop whether or not it can be repaired; with effort and ingenuity a spare part can be improvized.
· Make things last. Try not to be motivated by status and one-upmanship. If a product works and does the job intended, it need not be replaced by a new and often more expensive model, just for the sake of appearances.
· Avoid anything disposable when there is an alternative. Use cloth napkins instead of paper ones; china cups or mugs instead of plastic or paper ones; reusable nappies instead of disposable ones. Disposable goods almost always work out more expensive than non-disposables.
· Avoid impulse purchases. Carefully consider everything you buy. Do you really need it?

· Take a good look around your home. If an article is not used regularly (in other words, it serves a practical or aesthetic function), do you really need it? All those bits and pieces in boxes in the attic or under the stairs; all those clothes, stuffed in plastic bags, hanging in cupboards or sitting on the floor; all those books overflowing and falling off bookshelves – they have not been used for months or years, so why keep them? Better to give them to a jumble sale so they can go to someone else who may be able to use them.

FOOD

Three principles govern most food consumption in the North: we eat and drink too much; we waste a great deal; and too much of what we eat and drink is bad for us. Food is an environmental issue on four counts:

1. Land is needed to produce it, so the greater the demand for food the greater the demand for land to be converted to agriculture, and the greater the pressure on woodland and other natural habitats: over-consumption of food leads to over-consumption of land and increased pressure on the environment. Meeting the demands of the British diet is one of the driving forces behind agricultural intensification.
2. Eating habits have changed dramatically in the past 20 years, but the prevailing standard of nutrition is still poor. A great deal of the food produced to meet Northern demand is worthless junk food that uses up valuable agricultural land: because this type of food does not provide us with the nutrition we need, it reduces the effectiveness of the food supply industry.
3. A great deal of food ends up in household refuse; the average household in Britain throws away 130kg (290 lbs) of food every year.
4. Most agriculture depends on chemical fertilizers and pesticides to increase production, so much of the commercial food on the market has some artificial chemical content. The latter increases with the demand for convenience foods which encourage the use of artificial preservatives and colourings.

Over-nutrition is as much a problem in the North as undernutrition is in the South. As Erik Eckholm points out, it is the form of malnutrition that shortens lives among the rich.[9] A comparison of eating habits illustrates part of the problem. The North has a per capita protein intake nearly double that of the South. Differences between individual countries are even greater. It has been estimated that a 70kg (11 stone) man needs about 43 grams of protein per day, and a 58kg (9 stone) woman about 35 grams. Yet the average Briton has a daily protein intake of 91 grams, and the average American nearly 107 grams. By comparison, Kenyans have an intake of 57 grams, Indians 48 grams, and Bangladeshis 41 grams.[10] Figure 3 compares annual per capita British food consumption with that of Bangladesh.

The *Oxford English Dictionary* defines pollution as making foul or filthy, contaminating or defiling. On that basis, eating unhealthy or chemically contaminated food is self-inflicted pollution. There is growing evidence to suggest that there are links between the quantity and the quality of the food we eat and the high incidence of diseases largely peculiar to Western societies, notably heart diseases and cancers. Britons derive about 40 per cent of their calorie intake from fat and 20 per cent from processed sugar. Commercial cream of tomato soup, for instance, is 89 per cent fat and sugar; commercial ice cream 87 per cent; fruit-flavoured yoghurt 63 per cent; and digestive biscuits 53 per cent.[11] The incidence of heart disease and cancer has grown by 80 per cent in the UK since 1900. The consumption of sugar has grown by 1,000 per cent.[12] We consume too much fat, sugar, salt and alcohol, too little fibre and fresh fruit, and too few fresh vegetables. Nevertheless, eating habits have been changing for the better in the past 20 years, and are likely to continue changing as more research is done into nutrition and more people become aware of what is good for them.

	UK	Bangladesh
Sugar	40	3
Flour	60	18
Meat	73	3
Milk	125 litres	6 litres
Fat	26	—
Potatoes	105	7
Fresh fruit	35	6
Fresh vegetables	54	14
Beer	108 litres	—
Rice	2	120
Fish	6	9

Figure 3. *Annual per capita consumption of selected foods in the UK and Bangladesh (in kg)*

(Source: *Annual Abstract of Statistics* (UK) and *Statistical Yearbook of Bangladesh*)

The world as a whole derives two-thirds of its protein from vegetable products, and the rest from animal products. Vegetables are particularly favoured in the South. For example, Indians derive 90 per cent of their protein from vegetable products, Bangladeshis 87 per cent and Kenyans 75 per cent. By comparison, the North favours animal products. Americans derive 68 per cent of their protein intake from animal products, and Britons 60 per cent. Far more land is needed to support livestock than to grow vegetables or pulses. Twice as much land is given over to supporting livestock as to crops,[13] despite the lower contribution of animal protein to the human diet. There is still a prevailing misconception that adequate amounts of protein come only from meat. In fact, fish and eggs are better sources of protein because they are more easily digested. They are also cheaper than meat. Some fish (such as cod and halibut) are almost pure protein. Pulses are another important source of protein, and include many minerals and vitamins.

Another point to consider is the amount of energy it takes to produce food. Barbara Ward illustrated the point: 'Our bodies are fuelled by food, and the energy we get can be compared with the energy required to produce the food (in the form of labour, fuel for machines, fertilizers, and so on). A householder's vegetable plot – or an urban allotment – usually has an energy output of two to four times the amount of energy put into it. A Chinese farmer, with his intensive farming, can get an energy output forty times larger than his input. Wheat produced in Britain contains three to four times the energy it takes to produce it. In contrast, for intensively reared animals, the equation is reversed. Milk takes more than twice as much energy to produce as the consumer gets back in calories. Broiler meat passes on to the consumer only one-tenth of the energy invested in it. So does beef from feed lots. Commercial fishing operations can give back as little as a hundredth of the energy input.'[14]

The way we eat is generally determined by market forces, and market forces are generally determined by the way we eat. The prices of commercial food today are as low as they are because of mass marketing and free competition among manufacturers whose priority is to capture the biggest share of the market. In this system, minority demands play second fiddle. As a rule, the mass market has become used to dealing in unhealthy food. The result is that healthy food is that much more expensive because it is still sought only by a minority. This is why prices in most high street natural food shops are often higher. Manufacturers are picking up the move to healthier food, but making changes is a lengthy task that depends very much on identifying a firm market before investing in new manufacturing facilities and advertising. Most of the larger manufacturers need to be certain that changing demands are not just a passing fad.

The chemicals and artificial additives that appear in the food we eat are there partly as a result of the compulsion to use pesticides and chemical fertilizers to increase production to meet demand, partly because of the demand for convenience preserved food designed to look appetising, and partly because of the prevailing lack of knowledge of what constitutes a healthy diet. Almost all commercial crops in Britain are sprayed with pesticides, including several such as DDT, dieldrin and aldrin which are banned in the United States. Much of these pesticides remain as residues that are present in the food on our plates. The government reckons that occasional exposure to higher than average levels of pesticide residue in food is not a health risk, but this is debatable.

There are over 3,000 different additives currently in use, more than half of them for purely cosmetic reasons – to make food look and taste 'right'. In 1955, the average Briton ate 680 grams (22 ounces) of additives every year. Today, the figure is nearly 2.5kg (5 lbs 6 ozs), the weight equivalent of 22 aspirin-sized tablets every day.[15]

The amount of food that is produced, and the way it is processed and marketed, is a reflection of consumer demand. There are several ways in which the consumer can influence food production.

- Eat a balanced diet. This not only improves your health but makes efficient use of the food and drink you consume. A healthy and balanced diet means you derive the same level of nutrition from eating less food. Eating less food means less pressure on agricultural land, and so on the environment.
- Exploit the full nutritional value of food. Over-cooking destroys valuable nutrients. For instance, eggs are a good source of lecithin, a natural emulsifier which breaks down cholestorol. But frying or cooking them in oil destroys the lecithin; better to eat them boiled or baked.
- Vary your diet and sources of food. It is easy and tempting to be lazy and rely on the relatively limited selection of fresh and processed food available in food stores and supermarkets. This, however, encourages suppliers to continue supplying the same old staples, and, worse, to

breed them to meet what they regard as market demands.

· Encourage high street supermarkets by buying only their healthiest and most additive-free products. Instead of buying only from supermarkets, try buying fresh food direct from farm suppliers, or buy pulses, nuts, dried fruit, and food made without artificial additives. Buy organically grown fruit and vegetables and encourage organic farming. If the demand for healthy food grows, prices should come down and the availability should increase. High street supermarkets are already changing their marketing policies to meet the growing demand for natural foods without additives.

· Choose processed food with care. Always look at the list of ingredients printed on the pack and decide whether the preservatives, colourings, emulsifiers, etc are acceptable to you. For example, there is enough pure unsweetened fruit juice on the market to make the purchase of sweetened juice unnecessary – nearly two-thirds of the calories in sweetened fruit juice are in the form of added sugar. If the label does not list the ingredients, or if you are in any way doubtful, do not buy the product.

· As far as possible eat fresh food. This is not only healthier, but is preferable to eating frozen food (which needs electricity to run a freezer to store it, and often loses some of its nutritional value during freezing) and far preferable to eating processed food (which uses packaging wastefully, nearly always contains sweeteners, preservatives, emulsifiers, colourings or other chemicals, and may have been pre-cooked to the point where its nutritional value is reduced). Eating less processed food means less demand for packaging. As a rule, the less processed food you eat, the better.

· Produce your own food. Grow fruit and vegetables in the garden if you can, using organic gardening techniques. By making your own preserves you can eliminate the need for added preservatives and colouring, and regulate the proportion of sugar. If you make your own ice cream you can eliminate all the preservatives and artificial additives that are added to most commercial ice creams.

· Eat wild food. The countryside is the source of an almost bewildering supply of edible berries, mushrooms, nuts, herbs, leaves and ingredients for salads. On the coast of North Devon and South Wales you can collect laver, a nutritious and delicious seaweed. Delicious liqueurs can be made by using anything from sloe berries to beech leaves.

· Reduce or eliminate waste. The average British home throws out
2.5kg of vegetable waste every week. The passion for aesthetically
acceptable food on the table has long encouraged cooks to peel
vegetables, yet the skins are often the most nutritious part. Throwing
out peelings is needless waste. There should be no need to throw
away any edible food, least of all vegetables or fruit. Use only what
you need, and use any leftovers and inedible vegetable and fruit scraps
to build a compost heap for the garden.

ENERGY

After industry, the domestic sector is the second largest energy
consumer in the UK, accounting for half the gas and nearly 40 per cent
of the electricity consumed and for most of the peak energy demand that
influences planning for power station capacity. There have been sporadic
government attempts to encourage energy conservation, such as the
'Save It' campaign, launched in 1975 and abandoned in 1979. In 1983,
the Energy Efficiency Office was launched with a budget of £15 million
and the aim of cutting Britain's fuel bill by £7 billion per year. But
publicity and information campaigns are no substitute for regulation,
incentives or comprehensive financial assistance. Changes in Building
Regulations, for example, have helped reduce energy consumption in
new homes. The regulations on energy needs for water heating have
remained steady since 1965, but the regulations on space heating have
reduced the amount of energy needed by 40 per cent. In 1965, space
heating used 2.5 times more energy than water heating; today the two
are about the same.[16] The lack of incentives has still helped to encourage
British consumers to use more energy than they need.

According to *A Low Energy Strategy for the United Kingdom*, if existing
energy efficiency techniques were applied throughout the country, we
could cut energy consumption by more than one-half – at no cost to our
standard of living or level of economic activity.[17] Yet relatively few
British homes have taken effective conservation measures such as loft
insulation, draught proofing or double glazing. The result is that most
homes waste more energy than they use. About 50p in every £1 spent on
domestic fuel bills is thrown away – because the energy it buys is
wasted. There is huge potential here for individual consumer action.

Where does the energy used in the home go? The average British
household uses 64 per cent of its energy for space heating, 20 per cent

for water heating, 8 per cent for lighting and running electrical appliances, and 7 per cent for cooking. There have been two major changes in domestic energy consumption over the past 20 years. Firstly, consumption of solid fuels such as coal has fallen dramatically (from about 75 per cent to 20 per cent of the market share), and has been replaced mainly by gas (from less than 10 per cent to more than half) and electricity (which has doubled to 18 per cent). Secondly, the number of homes with central heating almost doubled between 1970 and 1980.

Reducing demand for energy has four major benefits: it reduces the need for new and bigger power stations, the need for expansion of the nuclear power industry, the consumption of fossil fuels, and the pollution generated by the energy industry (acid rain, atmospheric carbon dioxide, radioactive waste, oil spills, etc).

Heating

Space and water heating are not only the largest consumers of domestic energy (nearly 85 per cent), but also the most inefficient, mainly because of the lack of adequate insulation in most homes. In 1981, one home in four had no loft insulation and of the 13 million built since 1919 (and therefore most likely to have cavity walls), only half a million (4 per cent) had insulated cavity walls. Insulation and lagging could reduce heat losses by 30 per cent in flats and 40 per cent in houses, but a 1981 survey revealed that only about one-half of British homes had some form of energy conservation measure.[18]

The average centrally heated home uses about 30 to 35 per cent more fuel than a home with no central heating.[19] Yet many people install central heating without stopping to ask themselves whether they really need it, looking at energy conservation as an option, or considering its overall efficiency. Nearly two in every three homes are centrally heated. In many homes central heating is installed without adequate insulation or draught-proofing, and much of the heat disappears through windows, walls, doors, floors and ceilings. Some ventilation is essential to prevent dampness and stale air – one air change per hour is normally enough. But in the average Victorian house, ventilation changes the air about once every 20 minutes. This amounts to a considerable waste of energy that pushes up fuel bills. The difference made by cavity wall insulation to fuel costs in a semi-detached house is illustrated in Figure 4.

Cost of new central heating system:	Between £1,300 (electricity) and £2,000 (oil)
Cost of cavity wall insulation:	£300-£400
Annual running costs without CWI:	£320-£570
Annual running costs with CWI:	£230-£460
Cost savings of CWI:	20-30 per cent
CWI would pay for itself in three to eight years	

Figure 4: *Effect of cavity wall insulation (CWI) on fuel costs in an average semi-detached house*

(Source: Energy Efficiency Office, 1984)

There are several routes to cheaper and more efficient heating.

· Consider all the alternatives before installing central heating. Central heating is too often seen as essential, a first resort rather than a last resort. Double glazing is widely regarded as an accompaniment to central heating, rather than an alternative. One in three homes with central heating have double glazing, but only one in 12 without central heating have double glazing.[20] Yet, with efficient insulation and minimal heating, double glazing can keep most homes adequately warm. It can cost as much, or more, to install as central heating, but while central heating costs £300 to £600 per year to run, the only costs for double glazing might be small maintenance or repair costs.

· Regulate the use of central heating carefully, and make sure you are using it efficiently.

· Lower the temperature in the house. A temperature of 19°C (66.2°F) is reasonable for most needs, but many central heating systems are run at up to 23°C (73°F). The greater the difference between temperatures inside and outside a house, the greater the loss of heat through the fabric of the house.

· Heat only the rooms that you use most, and contain the heat in those rooms.

· Choose the most efficient and cost-effective form of heating. The efficiency of different heating systems is a crucial factor that people rarely consider. The traditional open coal fire, for example, while it looks very pleasant, is only 20 to 30 per cent efficient. The rest of the heat goes up the chimney. Solid fuel systems have improved markedly in recent years though, so that some new designs are 60 to 65 per cent efficient. In 1975, gas appliances were 62 per cent efficient for space heating and 54 per cent for water heating.[21] Electricity is the most efficient source of heat at the end-use point in the home or office, ranging from 65 to 75 per cent efficiency for night storage heaters to 100 per cent for electric fires. On average, electricity for heating is 86 per cent efficient.

· Exploit 'free heat gain' in the form of heat given off by lighting, electrical appliances, cookers, and people. With efficient insulation and control systems, and using the windows and walls in homes as passive solar collectors, it has been suggested that heating demands in schools, offices and other buildings heavily occupied could be reduced to *zero*.[22] In Canada, where winter temperatures can fall to 40° below and more, there are experimental homes that have no heating at all. They exist perfectly well on efficient insulation and free heat gain.

· Improve the efficiency of heating appliances so that less fuel is needed to produce the same heat output. Reflective foil behind radiators will retain heat that would normally be lost through the wall, and a shelf above a radiator sited beneath a window will deflect heat into the room.

· Use night storage heaters which run off Night Rate electricity.

· Install loft insulation and cavity wall insulation. More than three-quarters of British homes have lofts which could be insulated, but one in four still have no loft insulation. If all lofts were insulated, Britain would save the equivalent of 22 million barrels (three million tonnes) of oil, or 8 per cent of present domestic fuel consumption.[23]

· Use heavy curtains and insulated night shutters in winter.

· Reduce ventilation by draught stripping around doors and windows, blocking up unused fireplaces, adding an additional door in a passage to stop draughts, and building draught lobbies around external doors. This can reduce the air changes per hour from 3 to 1 in an average Victorian house.

Water heating

Water heating is the second major domestic energy consumer. Most homes use about 45 litres of hot water per person per day. Heating systems are often very inefficient, particularly if water tanks and pipes are unlagged. In a typical hot water system (see Figure 5), 31 per cent of the delivered energy is lost from the boiler, 14 per cent from the tank, and 7 per cent from pipes; in other words, more than half the energy

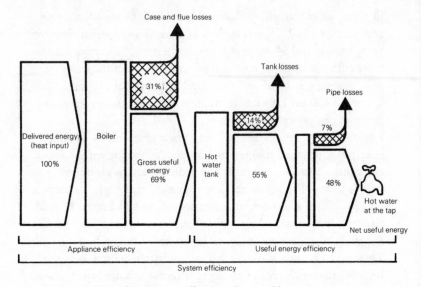

Figure 5: *Water heating energy efficiency with a central heating system*

(Source: Gerald Leach *et al*, *A Low Energy Strategy for the UK*, 1979)

used to heat water is lost before hot water comes out of your taps.[24]

- Make sure that tanks and pipes are lagged and insulated.
- Use a timing mechanism on your immersion heater. The average 3kW heater uses three units of electricity per hour. Leaving the heater on all night for a hot bath in the morning would use up 24 units of electricity. Switching on the heater with an automatic switch an hour before you got up would only use three units of electricity.
- A shower uses less water than a bath.

Cooking

Cooking accounts for about 7 per cent of domestic energy consumption, although this figure is declining slowly as more people use prepared foods and eat out. Gas and electric cookers are likely to become increasingly efficient. Research in Denmark in the 1970s showed that careful design (better insulated ovens and hot plates that responded faster) could cut the energy consumption of cookers by half, but until such cookers are on the market, the best the consumer can do is compare the energy consumption of different models when buying. For the time being, microwave ovens use 20 per cent less energy than conventional cookers.

- Use gas in preference to electricity for cooking. Gas ovens need no pre-heating, and gas flames on hot plates respond instantly to the controls. At January 1984 prices, a gas cooker cost £68 per year to run compared to £85 for an electric cooker.
- Use shorter cooking times. Cast-iron or glass saucepans retain and distribute heat more efficiently. The more vegetables are cooked, the more they lose their nutritional value, so shorter cooking times are preferable. Pressure cookers use much less energy to achieve the same ends as open saucepans. Slow cookers use the same amount of energy as a 100 watt light bulb, and also improve the flavour of the meal.
- Don't over-fill kettles or saucepans with water, and keep the lid on while cooking. Try cooking more than one vegetable in the same pan.
- Avoid opening the oven door during cooking, and try to cook as much in the same oven at once as possible. Grilling is the most energy-expensive method of cooking because most of the heat is convected up and away from the food.

Electricity

Electricity provides nearly one-quarter of the energy used in the average home (although the proportion can, of course, be as high as 100 per cent), and British homes between them account for nearly 29 per cent of national demand for electricity. Space and water heating are the major domestic electricity consumers, but lighting and electrical appliances can account for up to 38 per cent of domestic electricity consumption, most of it during the periods of peak load demand. Electricity demand as a whole is likely to increase as more people buy freezers, dishwashers, video recorders, and assorted convenience (largely non-essential) appliances. But even with more electrical appliances in the home, electricity consumption need not rise if the power is used efficiently.

- Take care with your electricity consumption. Most electrical appliances are labelled with their power rating, so the amount of electricity each appliance consumes can be accurately established. Electricity consumption is measured in kilowatt-hours (kWh), or the energy equivalent of one kilowatt (1,000 watts) running for one hour. At 1984 prices, a kilowatt-hour cost about 5p during peak daylight hours and about 2p at night. Your meter will also tell you how much you are using – making regular daily or weekly readings will give you a good idea of your consumption patterns. The key to

APPLIANCE	TYPICAL POWER RATING	TIME TAKEN TO USE 1 kWh	COST PER HOUR TO RUN (1984 FIGURES)	
			peak	night
Immersion heater	3kW	20 mins	15.0p	6.0p
Blow heater	2kW	30 mins	10.0p	4.0p
Toaster	1.4kW	43 mins	7.0p	2.8p
Power drill	360w	2 hrs 45 mins	1.8p	0.7p
Towel rail	250w	4 hours	1.3p	0.5p
Stereo system	180w	5 hrs 30 mins	0.9p	0.4p
Colour TV	140w	7 hrs 15 mins	0.7p	0.3p
Light bulb	100w	10 hours	0.5p	0.2p
Light bulb	60w	16 hrs 40 mins	0.3p	0.12p
Fridge	35w	29 hours	0.17p	0.07p

Figure 6: *Some typical consumption figures for electrical appliances*

cutting consumption is to tackle the big users such as immersion heaters, central heating and ovens. Making sure you switch off lights is useful, but a 100-watt light bulb takes ten hours to use one unit of electricity, compared to 20 minutes with a 3kW immersion heater.

· Be discriminating in your choice of electrical appliances. An electric can opener uses very little electricity, but is it really necessary? Many people use fridges as a larder rather than to store food that really needs refrigeration. Make do with a smaller fridge, keep it fully stocked, and keep it in good working order (check the door seals particularly).

· Review the usefulness of lighting and ask yourself whether everything is really needed. For example, do you really need to keep the porch light on all evening?

· Keep lights switched off unless they are really needed, and control immersion heaters and other big users with automatic controls.

· Keep windows and surfaces light in colour, thereby maximizing the use of daylight. Most British homes are draped liberally with lace curtains, even in upstairs rooms overlooked by no one. These reduce the amount of natural daylight entering a room.

· Keep light fixtures clean.

Gas

The use of natural gas in Britain has grown mainly since the discovery of gas in the North Sea in the late 1960s. Between 1965 and 1984, gas consumption rose by nearly 400 per cent, and it is still growing. More than 15 million households now use gas. In 1983-84 the total consumption for the UK was 17,300 million therms. Nearly 97 per cent of British Gas customers were domestic users, but they accounted for only just over half the gas used. Industry accounted for 33 per cent and commerce for 14 per cent. At the moment, Britain is almost self-sufficient in gas – the balance comes from Norway. But on the basis of known reserves, and given present patterns of gas consumption, British natural gas is likely to run out some time in the late 1990s. Gas would then have to be imported by pipeline. Prices will almost certainly rise and so will the British imports bill.

In the home, gas is used for central heating, water heating and cooking. Gas is the most popular fuel for central heating; a 1982 survey estimated that nearly two-thirds of homes with central heating ran on gas. Only 14 per cent used electricity. Although the gap between the cost of gas and electricity has been closing, gas is still the cheapest fuel for heating. To centrally heat fully and provide hot water for a semi-detached house would cost £321 per year with gas but £386 with electricity (at January 1984 prices). Although electricity is more efficient than gas at the point of the water heater or room heater, far less gas is lost in conversion and transport to the home. In terms of primary energy reaching the home, the figure of 93 per cent for gas is ahead of solid fuel (91 per cent) and oil (89 per cent), and far ahead of electricity (28 per cent).

APPLIANCE	TIME TAKEN TO USE ONE THERM	
	High setting	Low setting
Gas fire	5 hours	10 hours
Wall heater	10 hours	30 hours
Grill	7 hours	12 hours
Hotplate	9 hours	133 hours
Oven	20 hours (Mark 7)	36 hours (Mark 2)
Fridge	7 days	
Fridge/freezer	5 days	

Central heating and hot water for a two to three bedroomed terrace house use about 750 therms per year. A three bedroomed semi-detached house would use about 880 therms per year.

Figure 7: *Some typical consumption figures for gas appliances*

Many gas showrooms now have energy conservation advice centres. To use gas more efficiently, you can:

- Manage your gas consumption. The average home uses about 585 therms of gas per year, but in houses with gas central heating the figure is usually much higher. The average price of one therm is 35p.
- Keep central heating temperatures as low as possible. Reducing room thermostats by 2°C (4°F) can lower gas consumption by up to 10 per cent in an average household. Use central heating only when you need it, and use time controls. Lower the thermostat settings as far as possible when leaving home for more than two or three days.
- Service gas appliances regularly and keep them in good working order.
- On cooker hotplates, keep gas flames working at a medium setting that keeps them under the base of the saucepan.
- Use a new gas cooker without a pilot light. Pilot lights use a surprisingly large amount of gas. A large pilot light in a gas boiler could use as much as 2,000kWh per year, or 10 per cent of the annual energy consumption of the average British home.[25] New cookers now come with spark ignition, which has produced a large gas saving.

Alternative sources of energy

Advances in some new energy sources, notably solar energy, are progressing rapidly. At the present time, the applications are narrow and the costs still relatively high but, like computers, improved technology and ultimately mass production will bring costs down. A house can become a passive solar collector through the use of bigger windows on south-facing walls which collect the sun's heat, working on the same principle as a greenhouse. The conservation house at the National Centre for Alternative Technology at Machynlleth, Wales, uses one-fifth of the energy of a comparable size house by using insulation, quadruple glazing, controlled ventilation and a heat reclaim system that uses a heat pump. The use of solar water heating systems in Britain is growing slowly – among the larger schemes are the systems used by a group of 60 houses in London's East End and a group of 14 Victorian terraced houses in Southwark.

WATER

The result of Britain's abundant and cheap water supply is lavish and wasteful use. Water demand in Britain has grown by 50 per cent since

1961 (compared with a population growth of only 6 per cent). Estimating exactly how much water each consumer uses, and what they use it for, is difficult. The Water Authorities Association works on a figure of 125 litres (28 gallons) per person per day. This is used roughly as follows:

	LITRES (APPROX)
Lavatory flushing	35-39
Dish washing and cleaning	28-32
Bathing and showering	18-21
Laundry	14-16
Drinking and cooking	10-13
Gardening	3- 4
Car washing	1- 2

Figure 8: *Some typical water consumption figures*

All domestic water is treated to make it pure enough to drink, yet 90 per cent of it is flushed down the lavatory, used to wash dishes, clothes and cars, or sprinkled on to the lawn. Every year, each of us contaminates 13,000 litres (2,860 gallons) of water by flushing away just 550 litres (120 gallons) of human waste. The water that drains out of sinks and baths is contaminated with chemicals, detergents, solids and organic waste. It flows into the local sewers, increasing the volume of sewage and presenting local authorities with the problem of disposing of it.

This is just domestic use. When you consider that water is also used in many manufacturing processes to produce the goods that we demand, then each of us is actually responsible for the consumption of over 330 litres (73 gallons) of water every day. Producing a ton of paper, for example, uses between 90 and 270,000 litres (20 to 60,000 gallons) of water. Producing a tonne of steel uses about 205,000 litres (45,000 gallons). Electricity generating stations need vast quantities of water to cool steam used in their turbines. Much of the water used in industry leaves factories containing toxic pollutants and chemicals such as mercury and PCBs (polychlorinated biphenols, which are particularly highly-toxic and long-lived industrial chemicals).

In addition, supplying water affects the environment because reservoirs have to be built, often in the most beautiful parts of the uplands, and drawing off underground water can seriously deplete natural aquifers. The consumer has the power to ease Britain's water problems by reducing consumption, reducing the amount of waste water expelled into waste systems, and regulating the nature of that waste, that is, reducing the chemicals, detergents, and other contaminants in the water.

- Appreciate the value of fresh water and reduce consumption by imagining what it would be like to have to collect water every day from a standpipe or well – as is commonplace throughout the South – rather than having it readily on tap.
- Use a shower instead of a bath as often as you can. Whereas a bath might take 80 to 85 litres of water, a shower uses between 19 and 35 litres. Taking a bath should be an occasional luxury, not an everyday event.
- If it is not too big, water your garden with a watering-can rather than a sprinkler or a hose. Similarly, use a bucket of water and a sponge, not a hose, to wash your car.
- Lay a lawn over your garden, rather than paving which increases the amount of run-off into sewers.
- Collect rainwater in a tank (rather than letting it run down drains, thereby increasing the volume of sewage), and use it for washing or for watering the garden.
- Wash dishes only when there is a sink full rather than after every meal. Avoid using automatic dishwashers, which can use 50 litres (11 gallons) or more of water every time they are used.
- Reduce the amount of soap and detergent you expel with waste water. Washing-up liquids can be watered-down and achieve the same net result.
- Only run your washing machine or visit the launderette when you have a full load of clothes. Some washing machines use as much as 110 litres (24 gallons) of water per wash.

THE HOME

The national shortage of housing makes the renovation and conservation of existing homes very necessary. The National Federation of Housing Associations estimates that more than three million dwellings (14 per cent of the total) are in need of improvement and repairs costing more than £2,300. In 1982, renovation grants were given to more than one-quarter of a million dwellings. Renovation can turn run-down areas into desirable new suburbs – a well-known example of this is the London docklands. Restoring a house also makes good economic sense to anyone wanting a good return on his or her investment.

A Gallup poll, taken in August 1984, revealed that the Welsh led the country in the 'make do and mend' stakes. They were the most likely to repair broken household items – while more than 90 per cent of Scots would rather replace than repair. The Scots, on the other hand, are the most active supporters of energy conservation and repairing of rotting doors and draughty windows.[26]

The number of houses built annually in Britain has fallen from about 350,000 in the 1960s to 200,000 today. In the same period, the proportion of owner occupiers has risen from 41 per cent to an estimated 59 per cent, giving more people more freedom and incentive to repair and maintain their home.

· If you have time, buy an old house and renovate it in preference to buying a new house. Many dwellings qualify for a local authority or housing association improvement grant.
· Resist the temptation to replace fittings when they could be restored. Old sash windows could be stripped, repainted and fitted with new sash cords, rather than replaced with new windows out of character with the building. Old doors can be stripped and restored. Too much good material and equipment ends up deposited in skips or taken along to the municipal dump.
· Maintain a house and keep it in good repair. This will increase its value, extend its life and ease the demand for new housing stock.
· If you have a second home, try to make sure it is used as much as possible and share it with other people. Second homes in villages or the country may contribute to the run down of the area by denying accommodation to local residents, decreasing the local full-time population, and reducing demand for services.
· If there are few or no trees in your road, speak to your neighbours and get their support for approaching the local council to suggest trees be planted in the road.

WILDLIFE AND THE GARDEN

British wildlife has long had to exist within the confines created by humans. Hedgerows, woodland, verges, wetlands and seashores were, at least until the postwar intensification of agriculture, left relatively undisturbed. As these last pockets are now themselves increasingly threatened, so the value of private non-agricultural land increases. If you have a garden, no matter how small, you have direct control over a piece of the environment. There will be environmental problems against which you cannot guard, such as pollution, but apart from that you are free to determine how the land is used. You can curb the use of pesticides and encourage animal and plant life.

A drive or stroll through most suburban streets will reveal how many people there are who care little for gardening, shaking the belief that the British are a nation of gardeners. Certainly there are some spectacular private gardens, but many people prefer to concrete or pave their gardens, use them as a dumping ground, or simply let them grow wild. Letting them grow wild is perhaps better than nothing in terms of allowing nature to take its course, but the selective planting and cultivation of flowers and shrubs designed to attract birds, butterflies, insects and even small mammals such as hedgehogs and squirrels makes far more effective use of the garden.

Planning a garden to attract animal life needs an understanding of the feeding and breeding habits of the different species. The species attracted depend mainly on the locality of the garden, the size of the garden and the food plants available.

A pesticide-free garden

Pesticides are for lazy gardeners. There is almost nothing that can be achieved by pesticides that cannot be achieved by less pollutive and non-toxic means. Instead of spraying roses with chemicals to kill aphids, for example, dipping the buds in a bowl of soapy water will achieve the same effect. Pesticides not only contaminate gardens, but discourage and even kill the insects and birds that should be attracted to gardens. Spraying roses with aphid-killer may also kill the ladybirds that eat aphids. Chemicals will discourage bees and other winged insects from pollinating flowers.

The soil

The productivity of a garden ultimately depends upon the quality of the soil, a factor over which the gardener has considerable control. If the soil is too acid or alkaline the balance can be adjusted. Because plants are usually cropped or pruned, the nutrients they take from the soil are not always returned, so the gardener has to assure a supply of plant food.

The garden itself and the kitchen are ready sources – leaves, grass cuttings and pruned plant stems from the garden, and vegetable and fruit peelings from the kitchen can be decayed in a bin to provide compost (diseased plants, weeds and cuttings from hard plants such as roses should not be used; tea leaves, paper, cardboard and pet litter can be used).

Plants

Britain is rich in plant species but most gardeners select their plants from the limited range of popular species widely available from nurseries and garden centres. Most gardens contain plants that have been so thoroughly cross-bred for colour and larger blooms that they are far removed from their wild origins, and lack many of their natural features, notably scent. Many species are immediately rejected by most gardeners as 'weeds', a blanket condemnation which unhappily consigns many plant species to the dustbin. The philosophy behind too many gardens has traditionally been to create 'order' out of the wild profusion of nature, which leads many gardeners to sacrifice ecology on the altar of efficiency.

The basic principle behind the ecological garden should be to enhance, encourage and make the most of nature. Grow flowers such as roses for effect, but balance them with species that attract insects and birds and reinforce the garden ecosystem.

Insects

There are insects everywhere, and providing conditions suitable for moths, butterflies, bees and wasps is within the scope of even small urban gardens. Unfortunately, the relatively scentless modern hybrids of flowers grown for their colour and blooms often lack the power to attract butterflies and moths. Urban environments are less likely to attract most butterfly species than suburban or rural gardens. Butterflies need food and food plants where females can lay their eggs. For example, stinging nettles will attract small tortoiseshell and peacock butterflies, and grasses will attract the gatekeeper, the small heath, the speckled wood and the small skipper. 'Cottage' garden plants that will attract butterflies include buddleia, polyanthus, aubretia, lavender, petunias and primroses.

There are many plants that will attract bees, from common annuals such as marigolds and nasturtium to herbs like chives, thyme and sage.

Bumble bees can be encouraged by providing appropriate nests. Keeping a beehive is an ambitious but worthwhile undertaking.

Birds

There are three elements needed to attract birds to a garden: food, water and shelter. Providing food in winter is particularly crucial. Berries are a favourite natural food – barberry, cotoneaster, holly, viburnum, honeysuckle, etc. Most common British birds eat insects, seeds, berries, nuts and grain. Table scraps, puddings (oatmeal, seeds and nuts bound together with fat), fruit, and commercial bird food may also be eaten by birds. Regular provision of food at the same time each day (preferably early morning) will encourage birds to visit regularly. A reasonably broad bird table, out of reach of cats and squirrels and not built in a wide open space, will encourage birds; smaller birds will be attracted by a small feeder, such as a nut bag.

Possibly more important than food is water, for drinking and bathing. Provide a shallow pool or bird bath, again protected, if possible, from predators. Birds will be attracted by artificial nesting boxes. As the older trees in natural woodland, where many birds normally used to nest, become increasingly rare, so artificial nest boxes become more attractive to birds. Bird boxes can be bought or homemade. The simplest is a six-sided wooden box about 15cm wide, with an angled top and a hole 28mm in diameter (for smaller birds such as tree sparrows and blue tits) or 40mm in diameter (for larger birds such as house sparrows). Secure the nest box to a tree or the top of a post in a reasonably sheltered spot.

Ponds

The advent of the Save the Village Pond campaign was evidence of the concern felt at the disappearance of ponds. Building a garden pond helps to offset this deficit and is a useful contribution to the provision of freshwater habitats. A garden needs to be reasonably large to accommodate a pond, unless it is to be the main feature. It should be built away from trees and shade, and can be built either with concrete or polystyrene sheeting, or bought as a pre-formed glass fibre hull. The pond should be stocked with water plants (particularly oxygenators such as water crowfoot and willow moss) to encourage amphibians (frogs, toads, and newts) and insects (dragon flies, beetles and mayflies). Fish such as rudd and stickleback can be introduced if the pond is big enough.

Trees and hedges

Trees in a garden constitute a small ecosystem in themselves, providing support for a wide range of subsidiary animal and plant life. An oak, for example, will normally support up to 300 species of invertebrates.

The main factors to consider when planting garden trees is the type of soil required (beeches need mainly chalk soils, for example, and weeping willows grow poorly in clay soils), the size of the garden and the rate of growth of the tree. There should be no obstructions to their growth, either below the surface (for instance, foundations) or above (such as power lines, or buildings).

Planting a tree is a provision for the long term. Most trees take anything from 15 years (crab apple) to 100-150 years (oaks, beeches, elms, walnuts and yews) to mature. They also need considerable maintenance in their early years, especially if grown from seed. They need plenty of water, protection from damage, and regular pruning to encourage growth. The advantage of growing from an established tree bought from a nursery is that it is immediately visible and instantly provides food and shelter for birds and insects.

Hedges, too, provide habitat and shelter for insects, birds and small mammals, and are far preferable to sterile brick walls as borders around gardens. Again, soil is an important factor. The most rapidly growing mixed hedge varieties, such as Lawson's Cypress, will, with care, grow about 18 inches a year. Deciduous species such as copper beech take longer to grow than the fast growing evergreens but are worth the wait. Hawthorn and blackthorn grow fast, provide good sites for birds to build nests, attract winged insects, and provide fruit in the autumn.

Mammals

Attracting mammals to a garden is only really a viable proposition if you have a reasonably large garden and live close to open country, although smaller species such as hedgehogs and squirrels are regularly found in city gardens. The hedgehog is the most common garden mammal, and is a useful pest controller partial to hedge bottoms and herbaceous borders. Once found in the area, hedgehogs can be encouraged by regularly leaving out a plate of milk or by building a hedgehog home. Squirrels are attracted to gardens with enough trees to provide them with a year-long food supply – a two-hectare stand with well-established pines is usually the bare minimum. Among the more common garden mammals are moles, shrews, mice, weasels, voles, rabbits and, more rarely, bats, badgers and foxes.

REFERENCES

1 UN (1983) *Statistical Yearbook 1981*. UN, New York
2 Chandler, William U (1983) *Materials Recycling: The Virtue of Necessity*. Worldwatch Paper No 56, Washington DC
3 Ibid
4 British Paper and Board Federation
5 Chandler, William U (1983) op cit
6 *Glass Gazette* (1984) April
7 Hayes, Denis (1978) *Repairs, Reuse, Recycling – First Steps Toward a Sustainable Society*. Worldwatch Paper No 23, Washington DC
8 Chandler, William U (1983) *op cit*
9 Eckholm, Erik (1982) *Down to Earth*. Pluto Press, London
10 FAO (1983) *Production Yearbook 1982* Vol 36, FAO, Rome
11 Cannon, Geoffrey (1984) *The Food Scandal*. Century, London
12 Holford, Patrick (1983) *The Whole Food Manual*. Thorsons, Wellingborough
13 FAO (1983) *op cit*
14 Ward, Barbara (1979) *Progress For a Small Planet*. Penguin, Harmondsworth
15 *Green Drum* (1984) No 49
16 Heslop, DT and Sussex, AD (1984) *The new housing challenge – The reality*. Communication 1235, The Institution of Gas Engineers, London
17 Leach, Gerald *et al* (1979) *A Low Energy Strategy for the United Kingdom*. IIED, London
18 Surveys by Home Audit Division of Great Britain Ltd. Quoted in Leach, G *et al* (1979) *op cit*
19 Leach, G and Pellew, S (1982) *Energy Conservation in Housing*. IIED, London
20 Ibid
21 Leach, G *et al* (1979) *op cit*
22 Ibid
23 Leach, G and Pellew, S (1982) *op cit*
24 Leach, G *et al* (1979) *op cit*
25 Foley, Gerald (1976) *The Energy Question*. Penguin, Harmondsworth
26 *The Times* (1984) 20 August

OUTSIDE THE HOME

6

Waste and over-consumption in the home are curbed to a degree by
cost. Profligacy is a drain on the purse as well as on the environment.
But outside the home cost is often less of a restraint. In the workplace,
someone else is paying the bills. The state of the countryside is the
business of farmers and local residents. Holidays are for spending, eating
and drinking. Car drivers are usually unwilling to sacrifice their
independence and mobility in the interests of distant and intangible
threats to the environment.

In short, waste and over-consumption are often compounded outside the
home because people feel less answerable to themselves for the
consequences. Anyone who works in an office or shop will know how
paper and electricity are wasted. Anyone who has driven into the
countryside at the weekend will know of the jams and tailbacks that
come from too many cars on the road. Anyone who has gone on holiday
will know how tourism and commercialism can often spoil the local
environment.

IN THE WORKPLACE

First, a word about industry, the biggest national consumer of raw
materials. Industry consumes 37 per cent of Britain's electricity, 47 per
cent of its gas, 92 per cent of its coal, much of its water and oil, and all
its iron ore. It wastes the most energy and creates the most pollution.
The paths to making industry a more efficient user of natural resources
are many and complex, and beyond the scope of this book. But two
points should be emphasized. First, industrial activity is shaped very
largely by consumer demand. Industry does not always simply consume
natural resources, but, more often, processes them into a form
determined by consumer demand. Second, the working environment
within industry is ripe for change. Despite all the fuss about pollution,
many industries continue to pollute. British rivers in particular are

suffering. More than 2,800 km of rivers are too polluted to support fish life. Fifty years ago, the Mersey estuary offered a living to fishermen. Today it is devoid of fish. Cyanides, ammonia and other toxic material have left the Tees – the site of the largest chemical complex outside the United States – devoid of oxygen.[1]

Industrial processes frequently use energy inefficiently, and old industrial buildings and machinery are generally highly inefficient users of energy. Gerald Leach graphically described the problems of factory buildings: 'The typical industrial building is an energy conservation nightmare. It tends to have large doors and loading bays kept permanently open. It may well have broken skylights and windows jammed open. Since such buildings are generally six or seven metres high most of the hot air collects in the uninsulated roof space above the heads of the workforce while the heating system endeavours to maintain the appropriate temperature at ground level. Often, heating systems have no automatic controls. Extract ventilation systems are frequently kept running through the winter though their purpose is to provide summer cooling.'[2]

Space and water heating alone account for 15 per cent of total British industrial energy use. The bill could be cut by repairing holes in roofs, walls and windows, fitting flexible doors, fitting controls to heating systems, using units which circulate hot air back to ground level, controlling ventilation, insulating walls and roofs, and using temperature-controlled automatic switches. The use of combined heat and power (CHP) holds considerable potential for factories, offices and even blocks of flats. With CHP, a single device generates both heating and electrical power, the exhaust heat from the electricity generator being used for space heating. Factories and power stations could use this system to good effect. They could also capture waste heat from boilers and furnaces.

Making industry a more efficient user of natural resources, however, is a matter of changing policy, and requires considerable public and private investment. The consumer and the industrial employee can exert some influence for change, but the final decision must often be collective and made within the context of profit schedules and plans for the local or national economy. There is considerably more scope for the individual employer or employee in commerce to effect change because the costs and implementation of change are less of a constraint. Managers may argue that the time taken to arrange paper recycling in the office is not cost-effective. Offices more concerned with their image than their conservation record will willingly replace perfectly good furniture and fittings. Employees may feel that office spending is the concern of the accountant alone. But is it?

In fact costs at the workplace involve everyone who works there, and, with the larger organisations, the interests of the local community and the country are at stake. Company profits affect all employees directly, and the national economy indirectly. If profits are reduced by big energy bills and ineffective use of equipment, everyone is affected. The Energy Efficiency Office estimates that industry alone could save £1 billion a year if energy was used more economically.

Commerce uses about 60 per cent of its energy for space heating, 27 per cent for cooking and water heating, and 10 per cent for lighting. The proportion of energy provided by coal has fallen from 81 per cent to less than 10 per cent since 1950, and has been replaced by oil (44 per cent) and gas and electricity (22 per cent each). Many shops and offices are notoriously warm and stuffy, because they are both well insulated *and* well heated. Despite the fact that good insulation can remove the need for heating, radiators are often kept running on their highest setting, creating artificial, dry environments in offices.

Making adjustments to lighting and heating can be both cheap and easy, and produce major savings. Controls introduced by the government's Property Services Agency in 300 buildings in 1974 produced savings of between 30 and 50 per cent on heating and lighting. A Cambridge college limited its hot water temperatures to 50°C, reduced space heating temperatures, and encouraged everyone to close windows. Consequently, energy consumption fell by 44 per cent. A 600-pupil London school appointed 'energy monitors' who, by simply encouraging lights to be switched off and windows to be closed, reduced energy use by more than one-third.[3]

Heating
The same problems – and solutions – apply to offices and shops as to homes. Much of the energy used to heat space and water is wasted through inefficient heating systems and inadequate insulation. Improved controls, draught-proofing and better insulation all cost relatively little to install in that they can produce major savings on fuel bills. Offices also have considerable potential for free heat gain. People, electric

161

typewriters, wordprocessors, printers and photocopiers generate a considerable amount of heat during the day. Some of the larger photocopiers come with their own heat rating, which can be as high as 4,000 British Thermal Units (BTUs) per hour on standby and 5,000 BTU/hour during a copy run – the same heat output as a large radiator.

Lighting

Factories and industrial premises account for 37 per cent of electricity sales in Britain. Shops, offices and other commercial premises account for another 21 per cent. Demand from shops and offices has risen by nearly one-half in the past ten years. The Lighting Industry Federation (LIF) has an award scheme for savings in lighting which has encouraged factories and offices to achieve energy savings of up to 75 to 83 per cent by redesigning office layout, using more efficient and low-energy lamps, and maintaining their lighting systems. With lighting accounting for 45 per cent of the electricity bill in the commercial sector, many companies have found the systems paying for themselves in 12 to 18 months.

Introducing more efficient lighting equipment involves little or no capital expenditure, so the financial benefits are almost immediate. Where some capital outlay is needed the pay-back periods are usually short.

High pressure sodium lamps (or SON to give them their technical name) are the most efficient lamps available, giving 150 lumens of light for every watt of energy used (compared with the 12 lumens per watt given by domestic light bulbs) and generally lasting anything from 15,000 to 24,000 hours. Their applications are limited, though, by the fact that their output is monochromatic – everything they light appears as shades of orange. This still leaves them with many applications in industry, and they have been used to light games halls, swimming pools, golf driving ranges and tennis courts.

Among other kinds of lighting available:

- Metal halide (MBI) lamps produce about 80 lumens per watt (1m/w), although some types produce 120 lm/w. They last from 3,000 to 7,500 hours.
- The common 38mm tubular fluorescent lamp (MCF) can provide up to 90 lm/w or more, but 26mm krypton fluorescent lamps can provide the same light output at an energy saving of 7 to 10 per cent.

Their average life span is 7,500 hours, but this depends on how often they are switched on and off. The more they are switched, the shorter will be their life.

· Compact fluorescent lamps have uses in the home and the office. Some are available with bayonet mounts for use in table lamps. On average, they are four times cheaper to run than ordinary light bulbs, and last five times as long.

The LIF lists seven points for more efficient use of energy in lighting:

· Lighting levels should suit the tasks intended. The Chartered Institution of Building Services publishes a Code for Interior Lighting that gives advice relating to this.
· Light sources should emit colour suitable for the task. High pressure sodium lights, for example, should only be used where colour recognition is not important.
· Lights should give appropriate light distribution, casting light where it is needed and without glare.
· Using the maximum mounting height available for general lighting can be more efficient and less wasteful than low mounted lighting, and reduce glare.
· Local lighting can reduce the level of general lighting needed, concentrating light where the work is done.
· Lights should be installed where they can be reached for easy maintenance, and they should be regularly cleaned and replaced where necessary.
· Light colours on ceilings, walls and floors will improve lighting efficiency and reduce glare. Windows and skylights should be cleaned regularly to make best use of natural daylight.

Gas

Commerce accounts for 14 per cent of gas consumption and industry for 33 per cent. The potential for savings in consumption is illustrated by the roll-call of winners in the annual British Gas Energy Management Award scheme, designed to give public recognition to commercial and industrial organizations reducing their consumption of gas. In 1983, savings on gas consumption as high as 60 per cent and 72 per cent were achieved with a combination of new boilers, thermostatic valves, waste heat recovery, roof insulation, draught proofing, secondary glazing, more efficient heating systems and other conservation measures. One Ipswich company cut its consumption by one-third by recovering the heat generated by machinery, lighting and staff, mixing it with fresh air and recirculating it. Consumption in the twelfth century Guildhall in London was reduced by installing a control system which included weather-sensitive compensators that monitored and controlled the heating load according to the outside temperature. Improved furnaces and the use of a waste heat boiler have helped an iron works at Livingstone in Scotland cut its annual gas consumption by nearly 1.7 million therms.[4]

British Gas has itself been trying to use gas efficiently in its offices and showrooms. Between 1975 and 1979, one gas region spent £50,000 on conservation and produced cumulative savings of £1.4 million. In 1984, a British Gas board won the first Royal Institute of British Architects award for energy conservation. British Gas runs a research centre that investigates more efficient ways of using gas. Its Technical Consultancy Service will give advice to industrial and commercial companies on the methods available.

Paper

For most people the workplace is the major consumer of paper. Paper has long been the main medium of communication, through letters, reports, brochures, leaflets, catalogues, dossiers, files and computer printouts. Even a small office can work its way through prodigious quantities in a short time. Writing and printing paper makes up one-third of total British consumption.

· Institute a paper recycling scheme. Encourage people to put their waste paper in a separate container, and arrange regular collections from a waste-paper company. These companies will make collections as frequently as necessary and pay a nominal price per tonne. High quality computer paper is worth more than regular paper.

Business perks

Business perks have become the outlet for considerable waste and extravagance. The rise of the company car has encouraged increased (and usually unnecessary) traffic on the roads. With companies paying much of the mileage, there is even less compulsion for company car owners to reduce or regulate fuel consumption or worry about the wear and tear to their cars. Many cars are obviously used on the job, but many more are only used to drive to and from work in preference to public transport. They need parking lots to accommodate them; they use petrol inefficiently because they are usually driven slowly in heavy traffic with frequent gear changes; and they add to rush-hour traffic problems.

· Moderate the use of your company car. Drive to work only if you need the car for business or if no adequate public transport is available.
· Be discriminating in your use of business lunches and the company canteen. Free or subsidized food and drink is an invitation to over-consumption and waste, and often to health and weight problems.

TRANSPORT

Transport in this country has been revolutionized in the last three decades by the rise of the private car. In 1953, there were less than three million cars on the road. Today, there are 16 million, representing more than a 400 per cent increase (while population rose by just 12 per cent). Half the growth in energy demand between 1958 and 1979 was thanks to transport, and half of that to private transport. Thirty years ago, cars came second on the scale of most favoured transport, after buses and ahead of rail and bicycles. Today, three times as many kilometres are travelled in cars as in all other forms of land traffic put together. The problem of traffic on the roads is worsened by the fact that four-fifths of freight in Britain is moved by road. Furthermore, 99.3 per cent of transport is powered by oil.

The private car has become one of the most potent and ubiquitous symbols of the consumer society. More than with perhaps any other consumer product, patterns of car ownership are determined as much by status as by real need. About three in every five households now owns a car; the growth of private transport has been highest in the wealthiest households. The use of cars has roughly followed the price of petrol. After the 1973-74 oil crisis there was a sudden drop in use, followed by a gradual climb as the price of petrol eased off in real terms. But Gerald Leach points out that petrol only makes up about 30 to 40 per cent of total motoring costs, and that charging costs to company business has absorbed some of the shock of the price rises. In fact, it would probably take a 400 to 600 per cent rise in petrol prices to stop most motorists from driving as much as they do now.[5]

Cars are still far from fuel-efficient, partly because of body and engine design, and partly because of the way they are driven. Boasts that a car can run 40 or 50 miles on a gallon of petrol are meaningless when as little as 12 per cent of the fuel put into a car is actually converted into useful work at the wheels.[6] Nearly 62 per cent is expelled by the exhaust or used up in cylinder cooling. Much of the rest is lost in friction inside and outside the car, mainly through air drag and tyre drag. Cars driving in American cities were found to be either stationary or decelerating nearly 40 per cent of the time, using up petrol to no good effect. Devices to automatically switch off cars that are decelerating, coasting or idling are presently under development. Fuel consumption of most cars could be reduced by one-half, or more, with better design.

Fuel consumption can also be reduced if cars are used less, and used more efficiently – which is where the consumer comes in.

· Limit yourself to the minimum number of cars you really need. Preferably one per household.
· Use your car only when you really need it – as far as possible for pleasure only and not for work. Drive to work in a car only if the car is essential to your job. If you do need to drive to work, arrange car pools with neighbours or colleagues at work. Unless you really need a car, travel by train, bus or bicycle on holiday.
· Use a lighter car, as lighter cars generally use less fuel. A one-tonne vehicle will take about 18 litres (four gallons) of petrol to travel 100 miles. A 600kg vehicle will use only 11 litres (2.5 gallons).
· Look after your car and make it last. About a million cars are scrapped in the UK every year. Buying a new car every year or two is self-indulgent. New cars depreciate more rapidly than two-to-three-year-old cars, demand new raw materials, and add to the number of cars already on the road. It makes sense, both economically and environmentally, to buy a good second-hand car.
· Drive at a steady 90 kph (55 mph) to make the best use of petrol. Air resistance on a car travelling at 50 to 65 kph (30 to 40 mph) accounts for half the engine power; at 110 kph (70 mph) it accounts for 75 per cent. Although most people only reach high speeds on motorways, travelling at 90 kph instead of 110 kph can produce fuel savings of up to 18 per cent. In the US there is a blanket speed limit of 90 kph to which nearly everyone adheres. This has helped cut national petrol consumption there by one-fifth since 1978.
· Drive carefully and smoothly. Jerky use of the accelerator, sudden acceleration and constant gear changes use up more petrol, as does too much use of the choke.

- Keep your car well tuned. This will reduce petrol consumption and pollutive emissions.
- Fit steel-cased radial ply tyres instead of cross ply; this can cut tyre drag by a quarter, producing a 6 to 8 per cent fuel saving. Tyre drag is always present; at low speeds it is greater than air drag.
- Under- or over-inflation of tyres uses up more petrol. Correct inflation can mean a saving of one mile per gallon. Avoid sudden stops and starts.
- Avoid using a car for short journeys. Three in every five journeys made in Britain are of less than five kilometres (three miles); cars are used mainly for journeys of three kilometres (two miles) and longer. There is rarely any good reason for using a car for short journeys, especially where public transport is available.
- Use a bicycle, especially for short journeys. Bicycles are inexpensive, non-pollutive, quiet, take up little space, and provide healthy exercise. The amount of traffic on the road can make city cycling a hair-raising experience, but in the suburbs and in smaller towns or villages and the countryside bicycles are the ideal form of transport.
- Use public transport whenever you can. The arguments in favour of this are legion.
  - Public transport is more energy efficient. A standard two-way road can carry about 1,000 cars per hour or, at best, 5,000 people per hour (although, in reality, it is more like 1,500 people per hour); the same number of buses could carry 40,000 people per hour and a railway line up to 72,000 people per hour.
  - It is usually much faster, particularly during rush hours, and is nearly always more relaxing (barring strikes and delays).
  - It is less pollutive in that more passengers can be carried with less production of pollution per capita. Electric trains are the cleanest form of transport of all.
  - It reduces the need for more roads, car parks and supporting services.
  - It is safer. In 1983, 3,533 people were killed using private cars and motor cycles and only 278 using public transport. So your chances of dying in an accident are nearly 13 times greater with private transport.
  - It is quieter. If it is used for freight it can reduce the number of large and noisy lorries on the road.

IN THE COUNTRYSIDE

One of the main principles behind countryside conservation in Britain is the provision of amenity. Since the nineteenth century people have used the countryside increasingly for recreation and leisure. Preserving the balance between these demands and the demands of agriculture has long been a problem. The number of people using the countryside has grown apace with the ownership of private cars, which have made people more mobile, and the advent of longer holidays, which have given people more leisure time. (In 1960, most people had two weeks annual holiday; today most have three weeks or more.) At the same time, the area of countryside available for recreation and leisure has shrunk. For example, one-fifth of Exmoor's moorland alone has been turned over to farming since 1965.[7]

Despite the designation of national parks, AONBs and other areas in the interests of access to the countryside, very few have a public right of access. Although there are about 190,000km (120,000 miles) of public footpaths or rights of way in the UK, many have been created only through the work of pressure groups; some are deliberately obstructed by farmers; others are allowed to fall into neglect. There is public access to less than 3 per cent of national parks, and to one-quarter of one per cent of AONBs. Even commons are often closed to public access. Most people are aware of what is not permitted in the countryside in terms of where they cannot go and what they should not do, but there is very little guidance available on what people can do and where they can go.

Visiting the countryside is the most popular form of outdoor recreation. Every year at least three people in four make a trip to the countryside, which is more than visit the beach or stay in the garden. They drive, walk, climb, picnic, go boating or visit historic buildings. For most people these visits have one thing in common – they are unorganized. People prefer the freedom to move when and where they please and be their own guides. The vast majority of people visiting the countryside go by car. This gives them the freedom to travel at will. But it also causes traffic jams and tail-backs on major roads on weekends and holidays, and leaves the most popular sites surrounded by hectares of cars.

People are also creatures of habit and conformity. They tend to go where everyone else goes, do what everyone else does, and holiday at the same time as everyone else. A 1977 Countryside Commission survey spoke of the conservatism which 'inclines people to stick with the familiar and is reinforced by an uncertainty about where they can and cannot go in the countryside'.[8]

London provides an urban example of the tourist habit. The summer is the worst time of the year to visit the capital. It is jammed with tourists and traffic; prices are higher; accommodation is scarce; the theatres and restaurants are packed; and the weather (combined with car fumes) makes it often unpleasantly hot, muggy and dirty. Yet many people still feel the need to visit London during the peak tourist months of June to August, instead of going in April, May or September when the weather is cooler (but still often sunny), the air clearer, and there are fewer people. Parents, it is true, have their choices limited by school holidays; but even people without children feel compelled to holiday in August along with everyone else.

One of the side-effects of designating areas as national parks or AONBs is that many people feel that anything without such a designation cannot be so attractive. Yet some of the most beautiful parts of the country are not designated areas at all. The effect of everyone doing the same as everyone else is to put heavy pressure on the most popular parts of the countryside, thereby bringing about commercialization, despoliation and environmental problems. Stonehenge has had to be roped off to prevent damage from too many visitors. Land's End is criss-crossed with eroded footpaths from all the visitors. Britain's mountain peaks are crowded with people and sprinkled with litter.

- · Wherever you go on holiday, try to avoid the most popular areas during the peak tourist periods. Holiday in the spring and autumn as far as possible, when there are fewer people about and the weather can be superb, crisp and sunny. Try visiting places off the beaten track. As well as avoiding the rush, this can bring welcome custom to more remote country communities. Off-season holidays are not only cheaper but can reduce the effects of a sudden influx of visitors to the countryside during the peak summer months.
- · Try as far as possible to either leave your car at home or to leave it at the major centre of your holiday, and cycle, walk or take public transport around the area. Seeing the countryside from the inside of a car on a road jammed with other cars is not much fun. Cycling and

walking bring you closer to nature and the land and provide healthy exercise.

· Rather than keeping to motorways and A roads, pull off on to some of the smaller country lanes where there is little traffic and often superb countryside. Avoid the main roads, particularly during peak traffic periods.

· Follow the Country Code. This was first devised in 1957, since when it has been criticized for being too full of 'don'ts' rather than 'dos', and for advising visitors how to behave, but not local residents or farmers. Christopher Hall points out, for instance, that farmers are not encouraged to restore public footpaths after ploughing, to clean up any litter they create, or to avoid polluting rivers.[9] Nevertheless, the Country Code is a good general guide to how to avoid alienating farmers and help make the countryside more pleasant. The rest is common sense. The Country Code says you should:

   – Guard against all risk of fire.
   – Fasten all gates. Farm land is private land, and must be respected as such. A farm animal that wanders through an open gate can cause a road accident.
   – Keep dogs under proper control. Dogs on the loose can spread disease or worry farm animals. About 4,000 sheep alone are killed every year by dogs. Farmers are legally entitled to shoot dogs found worrying their animals.
   – Keep to the paths across farmland. This avoids any damage to crops.
   – Avoid damaging fences, hedges and walls.
   – Leave no litter.
   – Safeguard water supplies. Avoid polluting streams, many of which are the well-springs of local and regional water supplies.
   – Protect wildlife, wild plants and trees.
   – Go carefully on country roads.
   – Respect the life of the countryside.

As a general rule, the guidance given to visitors to many US national parks holds good everywhere: take only photographs, leave only footprints.

TOURISM

Tourism has a great deal to answer for. More commercialization, standardization, banality and environmental degradation is carried out in the name of tourism than possibly any other single activity. But it is all done to meet a demand, so the planners and the holiday companies cannot be held solely responsible. It is the individual tourist who creates the demand and frequents the facilities. Most tourists want to relax and enjoy themselves. For many this can include leaving hard decisions and moral arguments at home. They will visit a country with the object of exploiting the country's merits, and may demand better standards of food, accommodation and services than those they have at home. More often than not they take their custom to resorts and luxury hotels built to cater specifically for their needs, often at the expense of the local community. They rarely see, let alone meet, local people. Demand for such facilities can deny badly needed funds and resources to local people. It can mean that the local economy, society and environment become corrupted and upset in order to meet the demands of foreign visitors. Few tourists stop to question the justice or morality of this.

Britain is not only implicated in the export of such attitudes to other countries, but, as a major destination for tourists, suffers much of the same in return. Commercialization and banality have come to many of Britain's most popular holiday centres because of the demands both of Britons on holiday and foreign visitors. In 1983, nearly 12.5 million tourists visited Britain, an increase of over 60 per cent on 1973. Tourism has clearly made greatly increased demands on Britain's resources, but has also been highly lucrative. Earnings from the tourist trade in 1983 totalled more than £3.6 billion (up 400 per cent at current prices on 1973).[10]

While we may suffer commercialization, our social and environmental fabric is not as undermined or seriously affected as it is in many of the countries visited by Britons. During the annual August rush to the Mediterranean, for example, about 100 million visitors join the 100 million residents, doubling the demand for energy, food and water, doubling the output of sewage, and slowing down the progress made in recent years in cleaning up the Mediterranean. Coastal towns have adequate sewage treatment plants to cope with local needs, but not with the sudden tourist surge. Building additional facilities is hardly worthwhile for the few months in the year while the tourist season lasts.[11]

In the South, the position is worse. Tourism, it is true, can be used as a major argument in favour of conserving wildlife and creating national parks. Wildlife both benefits and suffers from tourism. Hotels, roads, water and electricity supplies are built in some of the most valuable wilderness areas, opening them up to tourist exploitation. Although trade in wildlife products is heavily controlled, many are still available. There are other forms of wildlife exploitation. In the tourist resorts of Spain and the Canary Islands until recently it was common to find beachside photographers offering to photograph visitors alongside a baby chimpanzee. In 1982, a trader could buy a one-to-two-year-old chimp for $5,000, and earn about $40,000 per year (tax free) from the trade. The chimps were imported from Sierra Leone and Guinea. The capture of a baby chimp could cost the lives of three to five adults, and many died during transportation. Once the chimps reached the age of five or six they were regarded as having outlived their usefulness and were usually destroyed.[12]

To alleviate the effects of tourism, you can:

· Respect the cultures and lifestyle of the countries you visit – when in Rome do as the Romans. Avoid corrupting local culture by imposing alien demands or demanding unrealistic services. The best way to experience the country you are visiting is to move with the country and its culture.
· Choose your accommodation carefully. A package holiday in large, foreign-owned hotels usually puts relatively little back into the local community as a whole, and may bolster the demand for prestige tourist developments which undermine the local environment. As far as possible make sure the money you spend goes back into the local community. Local people will benefit more if you patronize locally-owned hotels or guest-houses, eat at local restaurants, buy locally-made food, drink and other goods, and avoid tourist traps that eat up more in the way of energy and resources than they put back into the community.
· Avoid exporting wasteful and over-consumptive home habits to other countries. On the whole, holidaymakers save their money to go on an eating, drinking and buying binge. This puts heavy demands on local resources, and much of the money goes on imported food, drink and consumer goods.
· Resist the temptation to buy wildlife products. The argument that this will deny a living to local people who depend on the trade has little foundation. This trade is only a short-term solution to the problems of local people, and over the long term can harm them by

degrading the local environment. Local people are mainly responding to a perceived demand. If a demand is created for a different commodity, they will make a living from that commodity instead.

CAMPAIGNING

The argument that conservation is a brake on development and an obstacle to progress no longer holds any weight. It was fairly comprehensively rejected in the 1970s during the debate about how the human race was living beyond its means. Conservation does not mean going without. It means using resources and the environment rationally, positively and productively.

People are far less willing to accept the despoliation of their environment than they were a decade ago. There are still those in government, the civil service and the nationalized industries who think they know best about the needs of the community – and bring in squadrons of planners, scientists and engineers to support their arguments. But their claim to speak in the public interest has been increasingly discredited. They do not *always* know best. Crumbling high-rise blocks of flats standing in sterile urban landscapes, and motorway flyovers that dwarf people's homes and gardens, stand as monuments to some of the past weaknesses of government planning. Challenging public planning projects is not only a legal right but has repeatedly been shown to be an effective way of influencing change. Pressure groups have become increasingly adept at using the democratic process to respond, wherever possible, to government attempts to bulldoze public sentiment. The recent past is sprinkled with examples: the third London airport; the Vale of Beauvoir coal field; plans to gas badgers suspected of spreading bovine TB; and the Sizewell nuclear power plant inquiry.

Philip Lowe and Jane Goyder draw a detailed picture of environmental pressure groups in their book *Environmental Groups in British Politics*. They estimate that national and local environmental groups in the UK have a combined membership of about three million. Yet one of their principal conclusions is that environmental groups in the 1970s failed to translate this massive support into an appreciable political force. The result has been that, despite its successes, the environmental movement has achieved fewer institutional reforms than the smaller but more organized women's and consumer movements.

Influence and pressure for policy changes is exerted at two levels: national and local government.

National government

British government policy remains essentially unsympathetic to the environment, in contrast to the relatively high degree of environmental awareness and concern within the electorate – at least on some issues. An opinion poll in 1983 revealed that one Briton in two believed there was a serious risk of people using up the world's natural resources.[13] A survey in 1982 showed 64 per cent of people in favour of passing taxes to control pollution.[14] A poll at the height of the anti-lead in petrol campaign revealed that 80 per cent of people were prepared to pay more for lead-free petrol.[15] But the environment remains only a minor electoral issue, if it is raised at all outside the Ecology Party.

Successive British governments have proved remarkably slow to respond to citizen pressure for changes in environmental policy, although contacts between pressure groups and government departments are actively encouraged and pursued by both sides. The government may compromise on some issues or disputes, but there are enough instances of environmentally unsound government policies to cast doubts on any claims that environmental pressure groups successfully influence government policy. The government and its nationalized industries have yet to accept, for instance, that acid rain is a problem or that it is most likely caused by sulphur dioxide emissions from power stations, that nuclear power is widely regarded with concern and deep misgivings, that the widespread and growing use of pesticides could well have health risks, and that there is no need to wait for a European directive before introducing lead-free petrol. The inherent absurdities of the Wildlife and Countryside Act – the major piece of legislation on countryside management – stand as a monument to British government insensitivity. Government departments and nationalized industries may be reasonably accessible to pressure groups, but a sympathetic ear is no substitute for sympathetic action. A common complaint among pressure groups is that the government departments responsible for development 'listen to whatever we have to say, but only hear what suits them'.[16]

While environmental groups have received little sympathy from Whitehall, they have wider ranging support in Parliament. A survey of 74 groups found that all but 12 could rely on the help of at least one MP or peer, and that 19 groups had regular working contact with 30 or more MPs and peers.[17] These contacts are used to good effect – most of Britain's wildlife legislation has arisen through environmental groups sponsoring legislation with the co-operation of an MP. At the same time, though, the farming lobby in Parliament has enormous power. Only about 1 per cent of the population owns and farms land, but in 1972 nearly one in seven MPs either was or had been a landowner or farmer. Three-quarters of Mrs Thatcher's 1981 cabinet were landowners.[18]

Environmental groups do not as a rule have the power of sanctioning government plans because, unlike pressure groups in other areas, the government does not depend on their co-operation and so is not obliged to accommodate them.[19] Groups that become politically active have traditionally used two main weapons: public censure and delay. The former mobilizes public support for a case; the latter can be effected at various stages in the overall planning process, and has been used to good effect in motorway inquiries, for example. But delay and public censure can provoke government counter-measures. Not all environmental groups like to be associated with too much political lobbying for fear that it will affect their charitable status. Hence many rely on their political contacts and quiet behind-the-scenes negotiation.

Local government

The Town and Country Planning Act of 1946 made all development (except agriculture and forestry) subject to permission being obtained from local authorities. The authorities are obliged to draw up development plans to show how they intend to use the land in their area and to provide a blueprint for development decisions. These duties are divided between county councils (who produce structure plans, or general strategies for the county), and district councils (who produce more detailed local plans). District councils have the major say over development control. The system is designed to safeguard the economic, social and physical status of the area. One catch-all aspect of local planning is the provision of 'amenity', which covers everything from controlling pollution to providing a visually pleasing locality, protecting historic buildings, providing recreation, and designating nature reserves. The public has the right to comment and make representations on the local development plan.

Particularly since the late 1950s, county nature conservation trusts have built up both their membership and their expertise to the point where

175

they can exert considerable influence over local planning. More so than with national government, relations between pressure groups and local authorities often depend upon particular individuals. For instance, without the sympathy of the officer responsible, it may be difficult to persuade a local authority to join the national glass recycling scheme. If the local authority sees a pressure group as destructive or ill-qualified to comment, the group will work at a disadvantage. If the group can be seen to be working *with* the local authority rather than *against* it, the chances of success are greater. Lowe and Goyder point out that, because local environmental groups seldom become involved in supporting candidates for local elections, unlike ratepayers' and residents' associations, local authorities do not see them as a direct electoral challenge and so feel more amenable to their approaches.[20] At the same time, local councillors cannot ignore a well-supported and well-organized pressure group. To be seen to be working with the group can be good public relations for the local authority.

Local ad hoc campaigns, begun and supported by volunteers, can tap the groundswell of usually unexpressed support for environmental management and protection, and have proved an effective means of mobilizing opposition to a project. They have the advantage that local people can become involved in an issue that directly affects them.

The successful campaign to preserve the Gunnersbury triangle in west London as a nature reserve illustrates some of the possibilities. In 1982, British Rail and a development company requested permission to build industrial warehousing on a seven-acre plot of unused British Rail land in Chiswick, west London. The triangular plot was surrounded on three sides by railway lines, and had been idle since the 1930s, leaving it unusually rich in wildlife. Its birch and willow woodland supported 180 plant species, 30 bird species, 120 beetle species, and a family of foxes. The Chiswick Wildlife Group, a branch of the London Wildlife Trust, argued that the triangle should be preserved as a nature reserve, collected a petition of more than 3,000 signatures, and held public meetings that filled the Chiswick Town Hall. The Greater London Council gave its support, and the Chiswick Wildlife Group drew up a detailed report on the triangle's natural history. The Department of the Environment ruled against British Rail and the triangle has been preserved as a nature reserve. The GLC ecologist David Goode pointed out that, whereas the usual approach to nature conservation has relied heavily on comparing sites in terms of their intrinsic biological value, the Gunnersbury triangle issue was about the value of nature conservation in cities to local people.[21] The issue set an important precedent.

Campaigning is an effective and widely-available channel for expressing environmental concerns and influencing policy. If you feel moved to launch a campaign, a few basic principles are worth bearing in mind.

- Avoid duplication of effort. Before you start a campaign, check that an existing pressure group is not already active in the area. If it is, it might need support. If it is not, check whether members would be interested in lending their support to your project. You may achieve more by joining an existing body and mobilizing its members. The more support you can attract, the greater the impact and bargaining power of your campaign and the greater the chances of success.
- Organize well. This means working out a plan of action, composing a watertight case, seeking professional advice from friends or neighbours who may be lawyers, planners, journalists or local government officers, or hiring professionals if you have the money, and mobilizing public support. If you are trying to block a plan to build an office block or major road at the end of your street, form a local residents' association. Get people involved. Put leaflets through doors telling people what you are doing. Call a meeting of everyone in the area who might be interested and appoint a chairman, a secretary and a treasurer. Write letters to local and national newspapers, and encourage a local celebrity or dignitary to support you. Contact the National Council for Voluntary Organisations for their advice.
- Generate as much publicity as possible. Contact the local or national press, either directly or through press releases. Press releases can be an effective public force, provided they are well written and presented. They should be short, sharp and factual. They should give the five Ws and an H – who, what, when, where, why and how – in the first paragraph or two, be typed and double-spaced on one side of the paper, photocopied (preferably on letterhead) and contain a contact name, phone number and address. *Newsworthiness* is the key to attracting the interest of editors. Run publicity stunts. Do not let the story die. Keep up the momentum and keep in regular touch with your media contacts.
- Choose the right channels of protest. Find out what is needed, in

terms of planning or legal requirements, to lodge an objection to the subject of your campaign, and to whom you should object. It might be a private developer, the local council, the water board, or the electricity board. Stay within the set procedures of the law, and use the law to work in your favour. Research as much as you can to find out what laws and precedents you have on your side. Aim to work *with* developers or local councils rather than against them. Most will value the reflected glory of being seen to be working in the interests of the public good.

· Understand the other person's point of view. Development itself is not wrong, but development that degrades the environment or takes place at the expense of a reduction in people's quality of life must be disputed. If a local factory is the problem, understand the needs of the local economy and the provision of jobs. If a farmer is the problem, understand his priorities and make yourself familiar with his needs. Rather than simply trying to block a plan, present a well-reasoned and well-informed case on why the plan is undesirable and try to suggest some alternatives. Do not alienate the developer, but try to get him to see your point of view and at the least, compromise; at best, adapt the plan to ensure the security of the local environment.

· Involve your MP. Whether it is a local or national issue, he or she is there to represent your interests. It is an MP's duty to represent his or her constituents and, where necessary, to air your grievances either with the government department involved or in the House of Commons through a parliamentary question, requesting an adjournment debate, or referring the matter to the Parliamentary Commissioner for Administration, who must investigate complaints of maladministration when asked to by MPs on behalf of constituents.

If you have neither the time nor the resources for active campaigning, you might consider working for a voluntary organization.

WORKING FOR VOLUNTARY ORGANIZATIONS

Conservation, particularly in Britain, owes almost everything to the initiative of voluntary bodies – charities, pressure groups, and research institutes. Conservation was born out of the concern of private individuals, and it has only been through the work of pressure groups that most governments have adopted policies on the environment.

Voluntary groups still make most of the running in this country, whether they are one-person campaigns run from a front lounge or national organizations with multi-million pound incomes, regional offices, several hundred thousand members, and political influence. There are fund-raisers, landowners, political pressure groups, direct action groups, organizations running practical conservation projects, and weekenders banding together to save a village pond or rehabilitate a piece of derelict land.

National environmental groups comprise about 3,000 members on average, but the variation is huge. The Royal Society for the Protection of Birds (RSPB) has more than 300,000 members, and the National Trust over one million. Lowe and Goyder's survey found that people joined organizations for five main reasons: to register their support for the group's aims; to get the special benefits and privileges of membership; to get actively involved in voluntary work; to enjoy social contact; and to influence group policy.

Conversely, the benefits that groups derive from their members are: a source of income (by far the most important benefit), voluntary help, local watchdogs, a source of authority in dealing with government and others, spreading the word for the group, providing ideas, and giving active help in campaigns. On the whole, most groups see their members as sources of passive rather than active support, but the type of support varies very much according to the objectives of the group: some, such as the World Wildlife Fund, actively encourage members to fund-raise; some have no membership structure because of the costs and work involved in maintaining one, and prefer active individual involvement in campaigns; others, such as the Conservation Volunteers, exist almost exclusively to involve people in practical conservation work.

Finance is the critical factor, so most groups are first and foremost fund-raising charities. Most try to keep their running costs to a minimum, paying modest salaries and relying on the voluntary unpaid support of their members. Groups are only as good as their staff and their members, so efficient organization and active support and involvement of members are crucial. Lowe and Goyder found that many new groups closed through lack of efficient administration, and that many established groups were in danger of becoming too rigid and hierarchical. The quality of leadership has a major bearing on a group's effectiveness. The increased competition for available funds, coupled with a wider range of interests and priorities, has made many charities move beyond their roots and become more hard-headed about their work. In efforts to ensure its effectiveness, a charity must offer reasonable salaries to attract staff with professional abilities. The more a group is known for its expertise, the more likely it is to be consulted by government departments or the media. One national pressure group deliberately pays all its staff similar low salaries. While this appears to attract effective and experienced staff, it also means that turnover is high, continuity suffers and the group misses out on as many opportunities as it exploits, mainly because its staff are too over-worked to give their attention to everything. Low salaries are idealistic and a false economy.

High salaries, conversely, can attract people whose interests are far-removed from the grassroots support or aims of the organization. The small donor or the part-time enthusiast can be trampled in the rush to raise big money, attract thousands of members and generate political clout. So, while pensioners might make a considerable sacrifice to donate £2 to £3 to the charity, or a group of schoolchildren might work all week to raise £20, some charity staff may think nothing of spending the first sum on taking a taxi when they could have walked, or spending the second on a business lunch of dubious importance. Every so often, the less charitable side of even the most respected bodies comes to the surface, showing how charity leaders can often forget their obligations to grassroots support by over-spending, running excessive expense accounts, and incurring high 'administrative' costs. Recent revelations concerning the RSPCA provide a prime example. Recently, one major conservation charity is believed to have spent £200,000 on an office move of doubtful necessity, and to have made more than half its staff redundant when they opted not to move.

So, before committing yourself to supporting a charity or pressure group, check its credentials. What has it achieved? Is it cost-effective? Ask the group for a copy of its most recent annual accounts, and look particularly at the sums listed under 'administration and fund-raising', a catch-all heading often used to hide a multitude of sins. How much of the money it receives actually goes to the work it does? Is the money well spent? If it spends less than 10 per cent on administration it is doing very well. If it spends more than 30 per cent on administration it is time for questions. That means that more than 30p in every £1 the organization receives is being diverted from its target. If there are any doubts, phone or write to get a clear account. Keep on until you get a satisfactory answer. After all, it is *your* money and time you are going to donate. Such resources cannot be wasted.

REFERENCES

1 Pearce, Fred (1984) The great drain robbery. In *New Scientist* 15 March

2 Leach, Gerald *et al* (1979) *A Low Energy Strategy for the United Kingdom*. IIED, London

3 Ibid

4 GEM 83 (1983) *The Gas Energy Management Awards*. Benn, London

5 Leach, G *et al* (1979) *op cit*

6 Ibid

7 Shoard, Marion (1980) *The Theft of the Countryside*. Temple Smith, London

8 Countryside Commission (1978) *National Household Survey*. Countryside Commission, Cheltenham

9 Hall, Christopher (1980) Country Matters. In *Vole* February

10 British Tourist Authority

11 *New Scientist* (1984) 16 August

12 Anon (1982) The beach chimp trade in Spain. In *Traffic Bulletin*, IUCN Wildlife Trade Monitoring Unit, Vol IV, No 2, 23 July

13 MORI poll carried out for the Countryside Commission and WWF (1983)

14 Cotgrove, Stephen (1982) *Catastrophe or Cornucopia*. John Wiley, London

15 Wilson, Des (ed) (1984) *The Environmental Crisis*. Heinemann, London

16 Lowe, Philip and Goyder, Jane (1983) *Environmental Groups in Politics*. George Allen and Unwin, London

17 Ibid

18 Pye-Smith, C and Rose, C (1984) *Crisis and Conservation*. Penguin, Harmondsworth

19 Lowe and Goyder (1983) *op cit*

20 Ibid

21 Goode, David (1983) The Gunnersbury triangle: A new precedent for nature conservation. In *London Environmental Bulletin* Autumn, Vol 1, No 2

Postscript

TOWARDS THE SUSTAINABLE SOCIETY

'The only limit to our realization of tomorrow will be our doubts of today'.
Franklin D Roosevelt (1945)

'Human beings, in their quest for economic development and enjoyment of
the riches of nature, must come to terms with the reality of resource
limitation and the carrying capacity of ecosystems'.
World Conservation Strategy (1980)

Fifteen years ago, the North was worried about pollution, population
and disappearing wildlife – problems that were immediate, tangible,
emotional and which, above all, made good newspaper copy. But
population growth in itself was not a problem, and pollution and
disappearing wildlife were only symptoms. The fundamental problem
was – as it always has been – the relationship between people and
resources. Every environmental issue, whether acid rain or ozone
depletion, the extinction of a flower or the loss of a forest, ultimately
comes down to how we use natural resources. We can use them well, or
badly. We can manage them or waste them. We can be rational or
irrational. We can conserve or destroy.

For centuries, human exploitation of natural resources was taken for
granted. This is no longer so, and there is now little question that the
environment needs better care. Once that is accepted, only one question
remains: who is actually *responsible* for implementing this better care, for
taking the necessary corrective action?

'There can be no progress without the political will to change', is the
popular cry. 'All nations have to co-operate more urgently . . . in the
prevention of irreversible ecological damage', says the Brandt
Commission report. 'Prompt and vigorous changes in public policy
around the world are needed', says Global 2000. 'New levels of co-
operation among government, science, business, and groups of
concerned people' are needed, concluded the Global Possible Conference
held in Washington DC in 1984.

The underlying suggestion is that most people place the responsibility for change with their leaders. Nothing, however, is that simple. Harlan Cleveland observes that 'governments . . . are too responsible to take the responsibility for change'. Governments plan not for the long term, but only for the electoral term. Government is given power by the voter, so is a reflection of the community rather than vice versa. Reliance on 'top-down' solutions to environmental problems is misplaced.

Polls taken in the United States in the late 1970s revealed a low level of trust in the efforts of governments and industry to solve the problem of pollution.[1] The United Nations Environment Programme believes that the 1970s saw a general decline in confidence in the ability of national and international managerial systems to take effective action.[2] With or without public confidence, though, why *should* governments be expected to lead the way? Action is the sole preserve of government only where political decisions are involved. With the environment, many of the decisions are social rather than economic or political. Some decisions, it is true, cannot be taken by citizens (such as introducing lead-free petrol, expanding or contracting the nuclear power industry, and disposing of toxic wastes). For the rest, the citizen can act largely independently. Government inaction is no excuse for citizen complacence. Rather, the opposite is true. By withdrawing support for the unsustainable society, the citizen has direct personal power to influence how the environment is used.

In a 1982 survey in the Netherlands, nearly half those questioned felt that people themselves were primarily to blame for environmental degradation.[3] Erik Eckholm points out that 'citizen action – to identify and publicize issues, to press for responsible government policies, and work directly on environmental improvements – can help offset the myopic tendencies of government and industry'.[4]

One oft-expressed psychological barrier to citizen action is helplessness: what can one person or one family acting alone do to alleviate so wide a range of problems? Barbara Ward observed in 1979 that it can be 'very difficult to achieve and sustain a commitment to a cleaner, more appetizing and attractive environment if the scale of the problem is felt to surpass individual efforts while no collective clues or guidelines to an answer are provided'.[5] On the other hand, Robert Allen (compiler of the *World Conservation Strategy*) points out that no plan like the Strategy can work unless everyone becomes a conservationist: 'Personal attempts to conserve may appear inconsequential in relation to the enormous problems addressed in the[Strategy]...But such efforts are among the most significant of actions, the sum of which spread throughout society will mean real and enduring success'.[6]

Barbara Ward also observed that inaction often simply reflected not knowing what to do. This is becoming less of a barrier. As our understanding of the environment grows, so does the amount of information we have available upon which to base individual decisions. We daily know more about how human action affects the environment. We daily understand more about how individual demands can be adjusted. The British environmental movement alone has three million members – a solid foundation on which effective citizen action is being built. Taking positive action is not, however, dependent upon being part of a movement. The choices are individual, as is the decision to promote the sustainable society.

As Lester Brown points out, taking part in the creation of a sustainable society will be an extraordinarily satisfying experience: 'In effect, we have embarked on a shared adventure, the building of a society that has the potential to be an enduring one'.[7] For the industrialized North, the route to a sustainable future lies in using resources more moderately and more efficiently. It means a reappraisal of the way we live, and a questioning of the assumptions on which we base our current way of life.

The change has already begun. People are more aware now than at any time before of the need to conserve, and to use the environment rationally. The throwaway society is no longer viable, nor is it right. Disposability, waste, over-indulgence and planned obsolescence are indefensible; we cannot afford them. Neither can we afford to wait for a lead from government. It is individual demands which make up the collective action of communities and countries. We can change these demands, and build a sustainable future. The means are available, and the goal is clear. All that remains is for us to act.

REFERENCES

1 Althoff, P and Greig, W H (1977) Environmental pollution control: Two views from the general population. In *Environment and Behaviour*, 9, p 441

2 Holdgate, M W, Kassas, M, and White, G F (1982) *The World Environment 1972-1982*. Tycooly, Dublin
3 Ester, P (1982) How willing are the affluent to be ecologically responsible? In *UNU Newsletter*, December
4 Eckholm, Erik (1982) *Down to Earth*. Pluto Press, London
5 Ward, B (1979) *Progress for a Small Planet*. Penguin, Harmondsworth
6 Allen, Robert (1980) *How to Save the World*. Kogan Page, London
7 Brown, Lester (1981) *Building a Sustainable Society*. W W Norton, New York

USEFUL ADDRESSES

Most of the organizations listed on the following pages will provide further information and advice on their areas of interest. Many of the non-governmental organizations welcome voluntary help and involvement.

Key:
	MEM	Offers annual membership
	FUND	Fund-raising organization
	JOURN	Publishes regular journal/newsletter
	VOL	Voluntary/practical involvement offered
	LAND	Owns properties, reserves or collections
	EDUC	Runs an education programme
	PUBS	Runs a publication programme

NON-GOVERNMENTAL ORGANIZATIONS

British Association of Nature Conservationists (BANC)
c/o Carla Stanley
Rectory Farm
Stanton St John
Oxford OX9 1HF
Publishes *Ecos*, a quarterly journal which carries news and features on major conservation issues. Holds regular seminars and discussion on these issues.
MEM JOURN PUBS

British Naturalists Association
Willowfield
Boyneswood Road
Four Marks
Alton
Hampshire GU34 5EA
Tel: 04606 3659

186

Promotes contacts between naturalists in the UK and overseas, and encourages conservation of wildlife and natural beauty.

British Trust for Conservation Volunteers (BTCV)

36 St Mary's Street
Wallingford
Oxford OX10 0EU
Tel: 0491 39766

Organizes widely varied conservation projects around the UK and encourages volunteers to devote spare time to practical conservation.
MEM FUND JOURN VOL EDUC

British Trust for Ornithology

Beech Grove
Station Road
Tring
Hertfordshire HP23 5NR
Tel: 044282 3461

Promotes ornithology, with an emphasis on field work. Collects and analyses data from amateur and professional observers throughout the country.
JOURN VOL PUBS

Conservation Foundation

11a West Halkin Street
London SW1X 8JL
Tel: 01-235 1743

Encourages industry to support the aims of conservation. Publishes *Conservation Annual*.

Conservation Society

12a Guildford Street
Chertsey
Surrey KP16 9BQ
Tel: 09328 60975

Promotes public recognition of the limits of natural resources, and campaigns against environmentally degrading policies and attitudes.

Council for Environmental Conservation

c/o Zoological Society of London
Regent's Park
London NW1 4RY

Tel: 01-722 7111

Umbrella body for conservation groups in the UK. Publishes *Habitat*, a useful conservation newsletter, and offers information service.
MEM JOURN EDUC

Council for Environmental Education

School of Education
University of Reading
London Road
Reading RG1 5AQ

Tel: 0734 875234 ext 218

Promotes environmental education in the UK. More than 60 national organizations are members; CEE provides a forum for discussion of ideas, and runs information and publications services.
EDUC PUBS

Council for the Protection of Rural England (CPRE)

4 Hobart Place
London SW1W 0HY

Tel: 01-235 9481

Pressure group concerned with landscape conservation, transport and energy. More than 40 county-based branches. See page 124.
MEM FUND JOURN VOL PUBS

Council for the Protection of Rural Wales/ Cymdeithas Doigelu Harddwch Cymru

14 Broad Street
Welshpool
Powys SY21 7SD

Tel: 0938 2525

Equivalent for Wales.

Fauna and Flora Preservation Society

c/o Zoological Society of London
Regent's Park
London NW1 4RY

Tel: 01-586 0872

Raises money for the conservation of wildlife and habitats overseas.
MEM FUND JOURN

Field Studies Council

Preston Montford
Montford Bridge
Shrewsbury SY4 1HW

Tel: 0743 850674

Educational body which runs residential field courses on natural and
physical sciences, conservation, and land use and planning at centres in
England and Wales.
MEM JOURN VOL EDUC PUBS

Friends of the Earth

377 City Road
London EC1V 1NA

Tel: 01-837 0731

Pressure group that campaigns for the sustainable utilization of natural
resources. Runs campaigns on countryside conservation, energy,
transport, wildlife and waste. See pages 33-4.
MEM FUND JOURN VOL

Greenpeace

36 Graham Street
London N1 8LL

Tel: 01-251 3020

Direct action group that campaigns internationally against commercial
whaling and sealing, the dumping of toxic wastes, and nuclear weapons
tests. See page 34.
MEM FUND VOL

National Trust

36 Queen Anne's Gate
London SW1H 9AS

Tel: 01-222 9251

Buys or leases and conserves outstanding examples of the natural and
cultural heritage of England and Wales. See page 124.

MEM FUND JOURN VOL LAND EDUC

National Trust for Scotland

5 Charlotte Square
Edinburgh EH2 4DU

Tel: 031-226 5922

Equivalent body for Scotland.

Open Spaces Society

25a Bell Street
Henley-on-Thames
Oxford RG9 2BA

Tel: 0491 573535

Ramblers Association

1-5 Wandsworth Road
London SW8 2LJ

Tel: 01-582 6826

Campaigns to conserve and secure access to natural landscape. Principal
advocate of long-distance footpaths. More than 500 affiliated clubs.

MEM JOURN VOL PUBS

Royal Society for the Protection of Birds (RSPB)

The Lodge
Sandy
Bedfordshire SG19 2DL

Tel: 0767 80551

Raises money to conserve and protect wild birds. Owns and administers
reserves, and runs a public education programme. See page 124.

MEM FUND JOURN VOL LAND EDUC

Royal Society for Nature Conservation (RSNC)

The Green
Nettleham
Lincoln LN2 2NR
Tel: 0522 52326

Umbrella body for the UK's 42 county naturalists trusts, which between them manage more than 1,300 nature reserves. See page 124.
JOURN Through trusts: MEM FUND VOL LAND

Scottish Wildlife Trust

8 Dublin Street
Edinburgh EH1 3PP
Tel: 031-557 1525

Conserves Scottish wildlife by carrying out research, establishing wildlife reserves, encouraging public interest, and advising local authorities.
MEM FUND JOURN VOL LAND EDUC

Tree Council

35 Belgrave Square
London SW1X 8QN
Tel: 01-235 8854

Fosters the improvement of the environment through the planting, nurturing and cultivation of trees in rural and urban areas. Runs National Tree Week.
MEM FUND JOURN VOL EDUC

Wildfowl Trust

The New Grounds
Slimbridge
Gloucestershire GL2 7BT
Tel: 045389 333

Promotes the scientific study of wild and captive wildfowl, and maintains several reserves in England and Scotland.
MEM FUND JOURN LAND

Woodland Trust

36 Westgate
Grantham
Lincolnshire NG31 6LL

Tel: 0476 74297

Owns, protects and manages broadleaf woodland, planting one tree for every new member.

MEM FUND JOURN VOL LAND

World Wildlife Fund

11-13 Ockford Road
Godalming
Surrey GU7 1QU

Tel: 0468 20551

Raises money for the conservation of nature and natural resources in the UK and internationally. See page 124.

MEM FUND JOURN VOL EDUC

GOVERNMENT AND STATUTORY ORGANIZATIONS

Countryside Commission

John Dower House
Crescent Place
Cheltenham
Gloucestershire GL50 3RA

Tel: 0242 21381

Advisory body on amenity. Formulates policy for national parks in England and Wales. Provides grants for access to countryside, and helps in the creation and designation of country parks, AONBs and Heritage Coasts. See page 122.

JOURN EDUC PUBS

Countryside Commission for Scotland

Battleby
Redgorton
Perth PH1 3EW

Tel: 0783 27921

Equivalent body for Scotland.

Department of Energy

Thames House South
Millbank
London SW1P 4QJ
Tel: 01-211 6298

Responsible for UK energy resources, including energy conservation and management, and research into new forms of energy. See pages 122-3.

Department of the Environment

2 Marsham Street
London SW1P 3EB
Tel: 01-212 3434

Responsible for everything from local government to planning and housing – mainly people's living and working environment. Also responsible for environmental conservation, including policy on national parks, AONBs and pollution control. See pages 121-2.

Forestry Commission

231 Corstorphine Road
Edinburgh EH12 7A
Tel: 031-334 0303

Co-ordinates forestry management for industry; carries out forestry research; implements legislation; and monitors provision of recreational facilities and wildlife management in forests. See page 102.
EDUC LAND

Ministry of Agriculture, Fisheries and Food (MAFF)

Whitehall Place
London SW1A 2HH
Tel: 01-217 3000

Responsible for UK agricultural and fisheries policy. See page 123.

Natural Environment Research Council (NERC)

Polaris House
North Star Avenue
Swindon SN2 1EU
Tel: 0793 40101

Carries out research into all aspects of natural sciences. Several specialist institutes are members, including British Antarctic Survey, Institute of Terrestrial Ecology, and Sea Mammals Research Unit.

Nature Conservancy Council (NCC)

19-20 Belgrave Square
London SW1X 8BY

Tel: 01-235 3241

Advises government on nature conservation. Commissions research, gives grants, and manages Britain's National Nature Reserves.
See page 122.
EDUC PUBS LAND

Overseas Development Administration (ODA)

Eland House
Stag Place
London SW1E 5DH

Tel: 01-213 4953

Manages Britain's overseas aid programme, including capital aid and technical co-operation.
JOURN PUBS

Royal Commission on Environmental Pollution

Church House
Great Smith Street
London SW1P 3BL

Tel: 01-212 8620

Standing commission that advises on research into and control of environmental pollution.

Water Authorities Association

1 Queen Anne's Gate
London SW1H 9BT

Tel: 01-222 8111

Advises the government on national water policy.

NATIONALIZED INDUSTRIES

British Gas Corporation
59 Bryanston Street
London W1A 2AZ
Tel: 01-723 7030

British Steel Corporation
9 Albert Embankment
London SE1 7SN
Tel: 01-735 7654

Central Electricity Generating Board
Sudbury House
15 Newgate Street
London EC1A 7AU
Tel: 01-248 1202

National Coal Board
Hobart House
Grosvenor Place
London SW1X 7AE
Tel: 01-235 2020

INTERNATIONAL GOVERNMENTAL ORGANIZATIONS

Commonwealth Secretariat
Marlborough House
London SW1Y 5HX
Tel: 01-839 3411
EDUC PUBS

Council of Europe
Avenue de l'Europe
67 Strasbourg
France

Set up the European Committee for the Conservation of Nature and Natural Resources in 1962 to promote nature conservation in Europe. Publishes the journal *Naturopa*.

Environment and Consumer Protection Service
Commission of the European Communities
Rue de la Loi 200
B-1040 Brussels
Belgium

Food and Agriculture Organization of the UN (FAO)
Via delle Terme di Caracella
00100 Rome
Italy
Tel: 010 396 57971

International Bank for Reconstruction and Development (World Bank)
1818 H Street NW
Washington DC 20433
United States
Tel: 0101 202 477 2466/1234

International Maritime Organization
4 Albert Embankment
London SE1 7SR
Tel: 01-735 7611

United Nations Development Programme
1 United Nations Plaza
New York
NY 10017
United States

United Nations Educational, Scientific and Cultural Organization (UNESCO)
7 Place de Fontenoy
F-75700 Paris
France
Tel: 010 331 577 1610

United Nations Environment Programme (UNEP)
PO Box 30552
Nairobi
Kenya
Tel: 010 2542 333930/333610
See pages 93-4.

United Nations European Office
Palais des Nations
CH-1211 Geneva 10
Switzerland
Tel: 010 4122 346011

United Nations Headquarters
United Nations Plaza
New York
NY 10017
United States

United Nations Information Centre
Ship House
20 Buckingham Gate
London SW1E 6LB
Tel: 01-630 1981
UK centre for information on activities of all UN bodies.

World Health Organization
Avenue Appia
CH-1211 Geneva 27
Switzerland
Tel: 010 4122 91 21 11

Organization for Economic Co-operation and Development (OECD)
Environment Committee
Château de la Muette
2 rue André Pascal
75775 Paris Cedex 16
France
Tel: 010 331 502 1220

INTERNATIONAL NON-GOVERNMENTAL ORGANIZATIONS

Action Aid

PO Box 69
208 Upper Street
London N1 1RZ
Tel: 01-226 3383

Runs projects aimed at encouraging self-reliance in rural Third World areas.

FUND

British Volunteer Programme

22 Coleman Fields
London N1 7AG
Tel: 01-226 6616

Co-ordinates overseas volunteer service, currently sending about 800 volunteers annually to about 50 countries.

Members: Catholic Institute for International Relations
22 Coleman Fields
London N1 7AF
Tel: 01-354 0883

Voluntary Service Overseas
9 Belgrave Square
London SW1X 8PW
Tel: 01-235 5191

International Voluntary Service
53 Regent Road
Leicester LE1 6YL
Tel: 0533 541862

United Nations Association International Service
3 Whitehall Court
London SW1A 2EL
Tel: 01-930 2931

Catholic Fund for Overseas Development (Cafod)

2 Garden Close
Stockwell Road
London SW9 9TY

Tel: 01-735 9041

Official aid agency of the Catholic bishops of England and Wales.
Co-operates in self-help schemes overseas and runs information
programme in the UK.
EDUC

Centre for World Development Education (CWDE)

128 Buckingham Palace Road
London SW1W 9SH

Tel: 01-730 8332/3

Educational group which promotes knowledge and understanding in
Britain of world development issues.
EDUC PUBS

Christian Aid

PO Box No 1
London SW9 8BH

Tel: 01-733 5500

Official development and relief agency of British Council of Churches.
FUND EDUC PUBS

Earthscan

3 Endsleigh Street
London WC1H 0DD

Tel: 01-388 9541

Editorially independent news and information service on environment
and development. Publishes a series of paperbacks on key environmental
topics.
PUBS

European Environment Bureau

31 Rue Vautier
B-1040 Bruxelles
Belgium
Tel: 010 322 647 0199

Umbrella body for 60 European environmental NGOs. Monitors EEC activity on the environment.
JOURN PUBS

International Institute for Environment and Development (IIED)

3 Endsleigh Street
London WC1H 0DD

Tel: 01-388 2117

Policy research group which carries out studies on human settlements, forestry, energy and sustainable development.
PUBS

International Planned Parenthood Federation (IPPF)

18-20 Lower Regent Street
London SW1Y 4PW

Tel: 01-839 2911

Federation of national family planning associations which promotes concept of balance between population and natural resources.
JOURN EDUC

Overseas Development Institute (ODI)

10 Percy Street
London W1P 0JB

Tel: 01-580 7683

Policy research group which promotes discussion and exchange of information on economic and social development issues. Runs a comprehensive library.
JOURN PUBS

Oxfam

274 Banbury Road
Oxford OX2 7DZ

Tel: 0865 56777

Fund-raiser for relief and development programmes worldwide.
FUND EDUC PUBS

Population Concern

Margaret Pyke House
27-35 Mortimer Street
London W1N 7RJ

Tel: 01-637 9582

Promotes understanding of population issues and raises funds for voluntary family planning programmes worldwide.
FUND EDUC

International Union for Conservation of Nature and Natural Resources (IUCN)

Avenue du Mont Blanc
1196 Gland
Switzerland

Tel: 010 4122 64 19 24

See page 27.
JOURN PUBS

World Commission on Environment and Development

Palais Wilson
52 rue des Pâquis
1201 Geneva
Switzerland

Tel: 010 4122 32 71 17

Independent commission set up in 1984 under the chairmanship of former Norwegian Prime Minister Mrs Gro Harlem Brundtland to chart new strategies for tackling environment and development problems, and to increase public awareness of the issues.

World Resources Institute

1735 New York Avenue NW
Washington DC 20006
United States

Tel: 0101 202 638 6300

Policy research centre which analyses and provides information on global resources and population. Sponsored the Global Possible Conference in 1984.
PUBS

World Wildlife Fund

Avenue du Mont Blanc
1196 Gland
Switzerland
Tel: 010 4122 64 19 24

Raises funds through 26 national organizations for the conservation of nature and natural resources. Functions mainly through national organizations.
FUND JOURN PUBS

Worldwatch Institute

1776 Massachusetts Avenue NW
Washington DC 20036
United States
Tel: 0101 202 452 1999

Independent research group which analyses global environment and development problems, and publishes the authoritative Worldwatch Paper reports.
PUBS

SOURCES OF INFORMATION

Aluminium Federation Ltd

Broadway House
Calthorpe Road
Five Ways
Birmingham B15 1TN
Tel: 021-455 0311
Provides advice on aluminium recycling.

British Gas Technical Consultancy Service

Industrial and Commercial Sales Department
326 High Holborn
London WC1V 7PT
Tel: 01-242 0789
Provides advice to industry and commerce on more efficient use of gas. Will put inquirers in touch with local gas board consultancy service.

British Paper and Board Industry Federation
3 Plough Place
Fetter Lane
London EC4A 1AL
Tel: 01-353 5222

Provides advice and information on paper and board consumption and recycling.

British Plastics Federation
5 Belgrave Square
London SW1X 8PH
Tel: 01-235 9483

Provides advice on plastics consumption and recycling.

British Scrap Federation
16 High Street
Brampton
Huntingdon
Cambridgeshire PE18 8TU
Tel: 0480 55249

Energy Efficiency Office
Room 1312
Thames House South
Millbank
London SW1P 4QJ
Tel: 01-211 3000

Glass Manufacturers' Federation
19 Portland Place
London W1N 4BH
Tel: 01-580 6952

Provides advice on glass recycling. Co-ordinates Bottle Bank scheme.

Henry Doubleday Research Association

20 Convent Lane
Bocking
Braintree
Essex CN7 6RW
Tel: 0376 24083

Provides advice and information on organic gardening.

Lighting Industry Federation

Swan House
207 Balham High Road
London SW17 7BQ
Tel: 01-675 5432

Provides advice to commerce and industry on more efficient use of
lighting.

National Centre for Alternative Technology

Llwyngwern Quarry
Machynlleth
Powys FY20 9AZ
Tel: 0654 2400

Promotes use of alternative technology in heating and agriculture.

National Council of Voluntary Organizations

26 Bedford Square
London WC1B 3HU
Tel: 01-636 4066

Provides advice on the running of voluntary groups.

INDEX